NEW DIRECTIONS FOR STUDENT SERVICES

John H. Schuh, *Iowa State University*
EDITOR-IN-CHIEF

Elizabeth J. Whitt, *University of Iowa*
ASSOCIATE EDITOR

Meeting the Needs of African American Women

Mary F. Howard-Hamilton
Indiana University

EDITOR

D1270545

Number 104, Winter 2003

JOSSEY-BASS
San Francisco

MEETING THE NEEDS OF AFRICAN AMERICAN WOMEN
Mary F. Howard-Hamilton (ed.)
New Directions for Student Services, no. 104
John H. Schuh, Editor-in-Chief
Elizabeth J. Whitt, Associate Editor

NEW DIRECTIONS FOR STUDENT SERVICES (ISSN 0164-7970, e-ISSN 1536-0695) is part of The Jossey-Bass Higher and Adult Education Series and is published quarterly by Wiley Subscription Services, Inc., A Wiley Company, at Jossey-Bass, 989 Market Street, San Francisco, California 94103-1741. Periodicals Postage Paid at San Francisco, California, and at additional mailing offices. POSTMASTER: Send address changes to New Directions for Student Services, Jossey-Bass, 989 Market Street, San Francisco, California 94103-1741.

New Directions for Student Services is indexed in College Student Personnel Abstracts and Contents Pages in Education.

Microfilm copies of issues and articles are available in 16mm and 35mm, as well as microfiche in 105mm, through University Microfilms Inc., 300 North Zeeb Road, Ann Arbor, Michigan 48106-1346.

SUBSCRIPTIONS cost $75.00 for individuals and $160.00 for institutions, agencies, and libraries. See ordering information page at end of book.

EDITORIAL CORRESPONDENCE should be sent to the Editor-in-Chief, John H. Schuh, N 243 Lagomarcino Hall, Iowa State University, Ames, Iowa 50011

Cover photograph by Wernher Krutein/PHOTOVAULT © 1990.

Jossey-Bass Web address: www.josseybass.com

Contents

EDITOR'S NOTES

There are approximately 519,870,000 black women around the world. As Sharp (1993) says, "There's a Black woman on each of the seven continents, in almost every country and in the space program. So no matter where you go, she's already been there. She travels with forces greater than herself. Her presence is everywhere" (p. 7).

This quotation provides a clear image of the African American women who surround us on a daily basis. These are women who influence lives and prevail, often in the face of adversity; often they are seen but not heard. Their voices remain unheard because many people assume that issues that pertain to women in general or to African Americans in general pertain to African American women in the same ways.

The last *New Directions for Student Services* sourcebook that focused on the needs of college women, *Facilitating the Development of Women,* was published in 1985. In that sourcebook, only one chapter was devoted to addressing the special needs of minority women. Several paragraphs focused on four racial or ethnic groups as a collective and provided suggestions for programming for "minority women" in general (Evans, 1985). That source-book was, undoubtedly, groundbreaking, because few writers had focused on needs of women of color in higher education at that time. I note, regretfully, that many of the recommendations at the end of that 1985 chapter (for example, adequate funding, career planning and counseling geared specifically to women of color, more women faculty and administrators of color on college campuses) are echoed in this sourcebook. In addition, although the number of African American students on college campuses has grown exponentially over the past four decades, matriculation and retention challenges still exist.

More recently, in 1997, Michael Cuyjet edited a *New Directions for Student Services* sourcebook called *Helping African American Men Succeed in College* (Cuyjet, 1997). This was a major step in identifying within-group differences, as the sourcebook noted that experiences of African American men are unique, and the ways that they meet the challenges they face might be vastly different than those of African American women. Yet when research is conducted about African Americans in higher education, African American men and women often are treated as a monolithic group, thus masking potentially significant developmental and gender-related differences.

The purpose of this sourcebook, then, is twofold. First, we identify and explore critical needs of African American women as students, faculty, and administrators on college campuses. Second, we offer recommendations and suggestions for meeting those needs.

In Chapter One, Eboni Zamani provides a context for the rest of the sourcebook with an overview of the current status of African American women in higher education (in historically black institutions, community colleges, and public institutions). She also describes the similarities and differences among the settings and their implications for African American women.

Chapter Two introduces two theoretical frameworks, critical race theory and black feminist thought, which are rarely referred to when administrators and faculty attempt to interpret and address the challenges faced by African American women. Following an overview of the frameworks, I discuss ways in which the theories can be applied to practice.

Sherry Watt opens a discussion of developmental issues in Chapter Three by offering results of her research on identity and spiritual development of African American women. She describes spiritual connections that black women embrace in order to fight oppression, build resiliency, and strengthen their identity. Chapter Four continues the dialogue on interventions and methods for promoting a healthy identity for African American women. Authors Madonna Constantine and Tawanda Greer provide a case study and counseling techniques that can help African American women in higher education cope with the daily pressures of shifting from one identity—an African American woman—to an identity that may require her to assimilate and act in ways that are not part of her culture or psychological development.

Alexandria Rosales and Dawn Person explain the importance of programming support in the recruitment and retention of African American women students in Chapter Five. In Chapter Six, Lori Patton and Shaun Harper describe mentoring programs that help with academic challenges and preparation for careers. They offer many suggestions for campus policies and practice based on a qualitative study of the needs of African American women in graduate and professional school.

In Chapter Seven, Carol Patitu and Kandace Hinton describe the personal and professional experiences of African American women faculty and administrators on predominantly white campuses, based on two research studies conducted by the authors. The challenges these women face are often emotionally and intellectually debilitating, thus they choose to leave academia. Suggestions for recruiting and retaining African American women faculty and administrators are shared.

Where do we go from here? In Chapter Eight, Robin Hughes and I present challenges to change the existing campus environment for women. Also, changes in personal attitudes could open the dialogue between African American women and those who lack the desire to be supportive. Individual challenges and questions are presented.

Of course, African American women in higher education also are not a monolithic group; they have different challenges, concerns, contexts, and cultural heritages. Therefore, one must keep in mind when reading these chapters that one size does not fit all. Instead, this sourcebook is designed to begin the dialogue among and between all women who hope that their voices might be heard on college campuses and to validate the experiences they face. The eloquent title of Jeanne Noble's book, *Beautiful, Also, Are the Souls of My Black Sisters* (Noble, 1979), describes the contributors' hope for our sourcebook: we hope that the research and ideas shared here will challenge, inspire, motivate, and encourage you to promote the healthy development and souls of African American women.

Mary F. Howard-Hamilton
Editor

References

Cuyjet, M. J. (ed.). *Helping African American Men Succeed in College.* New Directions for Student Services, no. 80. San Francisco: Jossey-Bass, 1997.

Evans, N. J. (ed.). *Facilitating the Development of Women.* New Directions for Student Services, no. 29. San Francisco: Jossey-Bass, 1985.

Noble, J. *Beautiful, Also, Are the Souls of My Black Sisters.* Englewood Cliffs, N.J.: Prentice Hall, 1979.

Sharp, S. *Black Women for Beginners.* New York: Writers and Readers Publishing, 1993.

MARY F. HOWARD-HAMILTON is associate dean of graduate studies and associate professor in the Department of Educational Leadership and Policy Studies, Higher Education and Student Affairs Program, at the W. W. Wright School of Education, Indiana University–Bloomington. Formerly a student affairs administrator for thirteen years, she has work experience in special support services for disadvantaged students, multicultural affairs, judicial affairs, residence life, and orientation.

1

This chapter provides an overview of the historical roles and contemporary educational challenges and opportunities for African American women.

African American Women in Higher Education

Eboni M. Zamani

As the twenty-first century opened, the landscape of higher education appeared dissimilar from that of the past. One particularly visible change is in the composition of the college-going population: postsecondary institutions enroll increasing numbers of individuals from groups historically excluded from higher education because of their racial or ethnic background, socioeconomic class, or sex. For example, the National Center for Education Statistics reported in 2002 that minority students were roughly one-quarter of all undergraduates in 1989–90; in 1999–2000, that figure climbed approximately 8 percent, to over one-third, and is expected to continue to rise (National Center for Education Statistics, 2002). In fact, demographers project that by the year 2050, because an estimated 60 percent of the U.S. population will be people of color, members of so-called racial and ethnic minorities will make up the majority of students in college (Hobbs and Stoops, 2000).

African American students were 10.2 percent of undergraduates in 1989–90; this proportion increased slightly to 12.7 percent in 1999–2000. Student population trends also illustrate growth in the participation of women in higher education. In fact, attendance patterns indicate that for roughly thirty years, women's enrollment in higher education has been increasing at a faster rate than men's; women now account for 56.3 percent of undergraduates (National Center for Education Statistics, 2002). It is

---

In this volume, the term *African American* is used interchangeably with *black,* and in this chapter *two-year institution* is used interchangeably with *community college.*

New Directions for Student Services, no. 104, Winter 2003 © Wiley Periodicals, Inc.

very likely that undergraduate enrollment of women will continue to out-pace that of men (National Center for Education Statistics, 2002). This trend has particularly serious implications for African Americans. The *Journal of Blacks in Higher Education* ("Ominous Gender Gap," 1999) pro-jects that, if present attendance patterns continue, African American women will receive all baccalaureate degrees awarded to African Americans by the year 2097.

Despite the increasing proportion of African American students enrolling in postsecondary education, debates about the extent to which all college students have equal access to opportunities for success continue. For example, African American students are less likely to persist to degree completion than white students (Cross and Slater, 2001).

African American women hold a unique position as members of two groups that have been treated in a peripheral manner by postsecondary edu-cation (Moses, 1989). Membership in both marginalized groups often makes African American women invisible in colleges and universities. Given the complex intersection of race and gender, more attention should be paid to the educational, social, and political positions of African American women in postsecondary education.

This chapter examines the historical legacy of exclusion and the strug-gle for inclusion by African Americans in higher education and addresses the impact of race and sex on educational participation. Furthermore, the central aim of this chapter is to consider which types of postsecondary insti-tutions appear to afford African American women a sense of agency in meet-ing their educational needs.

The Intersection of Race and Gender

Across all levels, education has been gendered (Julia, 2000). The learning experiences of girls and women have been different from those of boys and men in terms of access to formal education, exclusion from various types of scholastic participation, bias in the curriculum, and instruction (Hayes, 2000b). All of these elements have contributed to overrepresentation of women in low-status, low-income-producing fields (Hayes, 2000b). At the same time, women's experiences have been very diverse, partly because they have been shaped by race (Julia, 2000).

For example, the women's movement of the 1970s, which sought to emancipate women, spoke primarily to the needs and concerns of middle-class white women, not to those of most African American women. The increased participation of African American women in the public workplace was opposed by white women in part because during and after slavery, African American women raised white children and kept white homes intact while dealing with their own family responsibilities (Lerner, 1992). It is not surprising, then, that African American women's welfare, concerns, or lack of participation in society were not a consideration in the evolution of early feminist thought. Therefore, "as far as many Blacks were concerned, the emergence of the women's movement couldn't have been more untimely or irrelevant" (Giddings, 1984, p. 299).

Although gender is salient in shaping identity and defining various facets of women's educational experiences, race also has an influence that often differentiates experiences and opportunities. Being female and African American places African American women at the confluence of two forms of oppression. This is the topic to which I turn next.

"Ain't I a Woman?" Historical Educational Disadvantages of African American Women

The history of African Americans is paradoxical because it is marked by movement from the antiquity of Africa, a rich ancestral heritage of kings and queens long before the Mayflower, through slavery, to Jim Crow and the present-day effects of previous discrimination and current racial prejudice (Bennett, 1998; Chafe, Gavins, and Korstad, 2001). The inequities faced by African Americans as a group have been particularly oppressive for black women. Lerner (1992) noted: "Black women have always been more conscious of and more handicapped by race oppression than by sex oppression. They have been subject to all the restrictions against Blacks and those against women. In no area of life have they ever been permitted to attain higher levels of status than white women" (p. xxii). This statement illustrates the place of African American women in U.S. society. Put more bluntly, African American women traditionally have been preceded by white men, white women, and African American men in importance and standing (Lerner, 1992).

The American system of education is a microcosm of the larger society, reflecting and reinforcing its strengths and flaws. Throughout the first two hundred years of the United States, the formal education of females was not universal. By the time of the Civil War, the literacy gap between men and women was bridged only in the increasingly urban Northeast, where middle- and upper-class white girls were taught to read and write (Lerner, 1993; Ogbu, 1990). African American men and women, as well as rural and immigrant white women, were not afforded the same opportunities (Lerner, 1993; Ogbu, 1990).

Over time, schools for special populations emerged (for example, historically black colleges and universities [HBCUs], single-sex institutions). Preeminent scholars and activists, such as Mary McLeod Bethune and W.E.B. DuBois, argued the advantages of voluntary segregation as an effective means of educational and economic attainment for African Americans, particularly African American women (Giddings, 1984).

Today, African Americans are enrolled in K–16 education in record numbers, yet the increase in higher education attendance has been slow, and the status of African American students remains relatively unchanged (Zamani and Brown, 2003). Although higher education demonstrates

Table 1.1. African American College Enrollment by Gender, 1980 and 1999

	1980		1999	
	Men	Women	Men	Women
Total	463,700	643,000	603,000	1,037,700
Percentage	42%	58%	36.8%	63.2%

Source: U.S. Department of Education, 1999.

considerable student diversity compared to the past, institutions of higher education have yet to mirror societal pluralism (Zamani and Brown, 2003). For example, African Americans account for 12.5 percent of the general population, but an estimated 11 percent of the total college student population is composed of African Americans. In addition, many African American college students attend lower-prestige institutions, such as community colleges and regional state universities (Altbach, Lomotey, and Rivers, 2002; U.S. Department of Education, 1999). And although African American student enrollment has increased, an examination of college attendance patterns by sex (Table 1.1) yields interesting within-group trends.

Literature on student participation in postsecondary education by race or ethnicity consistently reveals higher rates of college participation and completion among African American women than African American men (Gregory, 1999; "Ominous Gender Gap," 1999; "Troublesome Decline," 2001). Nearly two-thirds of African American undergraduates are women (*Journal of Blacks in Higher Education,* 1999). According to Trent (1991), a feminization of African American education is occurring, which has serious implications for distribution of jobs as well as selection of mates.

Between 1976 and 1999, African American students increased from 6 to 9 percent of total enrollment in graduate programs and from 5 to 8 percent in first professional programs (National Center for Education Statistics, 2002). Modest enrollment increases for African Americans at the graduate level as a group can be attributed to the enrollment of African American women in larger numbers (Ruffins, 1997). From these statistics, it is evident that a gender gap in educational attainment occurs among African Americans that does not appear to the same degree in other racial or ethnic groups (Malveaux, 2002).

In addition, despite increases in African American participation in higher education, formal and informal barriers to persistence, including a postsecondary education system stratified by socioeconomic status, persist (Altbach, Lomotey, and Rivers, 2002). These barriers are particularly salient for African American women, who continue to suffer the effects of gender and racial bias (Bowman, 1995; Hayes, 2000a, 2000b).

In addition, as the percentage of African American males in higher education decreased, the actual number of African American males remained stable while larger numbers of African American women attended higher learning institutions. African American women often are put in the position of representing their race to a predominantly white system (Turner, 2001). In further elucidating African American women's status, Malveaux (1998) reveals that, on average, a college education afforded white women a 4.4 percent increase in wages; African American female college graduates' earnings were 3.2 percent lower than white female counterparts. Frequently, African American women are disproportionately affected by wage differentials or gaps (Malveaux, 1998). For this reason and others, it is essential to assess the divergent educational contexts that African American women occupy, to determine which environments foster and which inhibit success for collegiate African American women.

Institutional Type: Addressing Variation in Higher Education Environments

"The value African Americans place on education has always been extraordinarily high. There is a deep historical and cultural belief in the efficacy of education. Blacks have sought education in every conceivable manner at every level" (Billingsley, 1992, p. 181). Given the diversity in student populations across colleges and universities, issues of race and gender vary by institutional context. Therefore, it is very important to examine not only *if* African American students enter college but *where* they enter (see Figure 1.1).

Segregation in higher education continues; most African American students enroll in institutions considered to be of low status, including two-year colleges (Renner, 2003; Zamani and Brown, 2003). The large number of African Americans at community colleges is especially problematic if their educational goals include more than an associate degree; students who enter a two-year college intending eventually to obtain a bachelor's degree are less likely to attain that goal than those who enter a four-year college (Brint and Karabel, 1989; Dougherty, 1994; Pascarella and others, 1998; Pincus and Archer, 1989). Renner contends, "numerically, minority students are less equal now than they were thirty years ago on the criterion that really matters, college graduation" (2003, p. 40). Given the demographic shifts in the general population, however, it is in the country's best interest to increase the college participation of African Americans, women, and other persons of color across all institutional types, particularly selective colleges and universities as fewer whites (white men in particular) will comprise the workforce in the next couple of decades.

Because it is likely that self-concepts and experiences of African American women are influenced by the composition—by sex and by race—of the colleges they attend (Aragon and Zamani, 2002; Jackson, 1998), the

Figure 1.1. Percentage Distribution of African American Student Enrollment at Two-Year and Four-Year Institutions

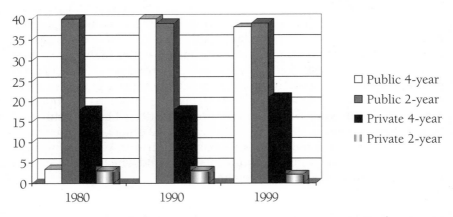

Source: U.S. Department of Education, 1999.

missions, characteristics, and climates of postsecondary institutions require attention with regard to their capacity to foster postsecondary educational attainment for African American women. The institutional mission reflects a stated purpose and enduring vision that directs and distinguishes a college or university (Peeke, 1994). Moreover, the mission shapes the institutional context and the campus ecology (the person-environment fit within the college setting), which directly influence goodness of fit or match between the student and the institution (Sinton, 1996).

African American college students do not attend higher-status institutions, such as research universities and Ivy League colleges, to the same degree as their white peers, and it is arguable whether institutions of that kind are the most successful in fostering the advancement of African American students in general and African American women in particular. Research by Wolf-Wendel (1998) asserts that although predominantly white, elite institutions receive the most acclaim for student outcomes, colleges for special populations (for example, HBCUs and women's colleges) should be given more credit, because they account for a greater proportion of African American and women achievers.

Other researchers have argued that institutional cultures and campus climates at HBCUs and other minority-serving institutions are perceived as more welcoming to students of color than are predominantly white institutions (Brown and Davis, 2001; Hurtado, Milem, and Clayton-Pedersen, 1999). For the most part, institutions that have a mission dedicated to underserved or marginalized groups might be thought to have a better appreciation for students' backgrounds and needs and, therefore, to provide the student with a level of cultural capital that he or she might not obtain at a majority-serving college or university.

Historically Black Colleges and Universities and Predominantly White Institutions. Although it was illegal to educate persons of African descent in many parts of this country until after the Civil War, foundations were established for the education of African Americans (Bowman, 1992). In the late 1800s, only a relatively small number of white institutions admitted African Americans, and those that did were located primarily in the North; however, the majority of African Americans resided in the South (Guyden, 1999). Legal racial separation of colleges and universities was launched (particularly in the South) with the second Morrill Act of 1890, which established public land-grant institutions of higher education for African Americans. Most of these new colleges were four-year institutions (Cohen, 1998).

As a group, the "1890 universities" and their private college counterparts often are referred to as historically black colleges and universities. Most of these institutions were located in small towns and rural areas of the South and were affiliated with a religious denomination (Clayton, 1979). Because the initial mission of HBCUs was to improve the economic and social conditions of newly freed slaves, their curricula originally had a vocational emphasis. Over time, that emphasis evolved to include and promote general education and liberal arts (Drewry and Doermann, 2001; Gray, 2001; Guyden, 1999).

Today, there are an estimated 103 HBCUs in the United States, which enroll 16 percent of African American college students. Thus, HBCUs constitute 3 percent of all American postsecondary institutions and 9 percent of baccalaureate degree–granting colleges and universities (Bowman, 1992; Gray, 2001; Hope, 1996; Wagener and Nettles, 1998). Although well over 80 percent of African American students attend predominantly white institutions (PWIs), HBCUs have consistently produced slightly over one-third of African American degree recipients, more than other institutional types (Hope, 1996; Wolf-Wendel, 1998).

There are significant differences in the educational outcomes of African American students (especially African American women) at HBCUs than those at PWIs. Chief among these differences is the extent to which HBCUs foster degree aspirations and encourage careers in engineering, the natural sciences, or mathematics (Carter, 2001; Chenoweth, 1997; Grandy, 1998; Joiner, 2001). In addition, studies have found that HBCUs are more efficient and productive than PWIs in terms of expenditures per student; operating with fewer fiscal resources than majority schools, they produce the majority of black college graduates that go on to receive Ph.D.s (Wolf-Wendel, 1998; Wolf-Wendel, Blacker, and Morphew, 2000). In fact, of the twenty institutions of higher education that graduate the highest number of African American students who later earn doctorates, nine are HBCUs (Gray, 2001). African American women outnumber African American men at both PWIs and HBCUs (Drewry and Doermann, 2001). However, for African American women, attending an HBCU can greatly benefit their development and positively affect academic performance and subsequent mobility (Jackson and Swan, 1991; Wolf-Wendel, 1998).

Similar to historically black four-year institutions, historically black two-year colleges (HBCs) carried the charge to provide ex-slaves with educational opportunities. Unlike historically black four-year colleges and universities, however, the development of black two-year institutions was largely an outgrowth of the twentieth century (Guyden, 1999). Also, black two-year institutions largely promoted a liberal arts curriculum with the purpose of encouraging transfer in pursuit of baccalaureate degrees. At one time, more than one hundred black colleges were two-year institutions or provided two-year curricula; only fourteen historically black two-year institutions remained by 1997, most located in the Southeast (*Historically Black Colleges and Universities Fact Book*, 1983).

As noted earlier, HBCUs were originated solely for the purpose of educating African Americans. However, over time predominantly black institutions (PBIs) have emerged from predominantly white institutions that experienced significant growth in enrollments of African American students (Guyden, 1999; Townsend, 1999). Both two-year and four-year PBIs are typically located in major cities in which at least 50 percent of the population is African American (Townsend, 1999).

Community Colleges and Proprietary Postsecondary Institutions. Community college students are among the most diverse collegiate populations in the United States. The vast majority of educational opportunities for students of color have been at two-year institutions, despite the fact that students of color typically have higher educational aspirations than their white counterparts (Carter, 1999, 2001; Cohen and Brawer, 2003).

Community colleges play a significant role in providing educational access and opportunity to minority students. Every fall, about half of all undergraduate students of color enroll in community colleges. Roughly two-fifths of African Americans are in two-year institutions, and the majority of these students are women (Phillippe and Patton, 2000). In addition, 58 percent of all community college students are women, three-fourths of whom attend on a part-time basis (Phillippe and Patton, 2000; White, 2001).

Of students at community colleges, women receive the largest number of associate degrees and certificates. Nonetheless, it is debatable whether community colleges are the most practical educational option for African American women students who might not otherwise have postsecondary opportunities. For example, white students are more likely than African American students to obtain two-year degrees and certificates.

As with community colleges, important contributions to educational access have been made by private, for-profit postsecondary institutions. Conveniently located in urban areas close to where many students of color work or live, proprietary institutions are becoming key providers of postsecondary degree programs, drawing increasing numbers of African

American women and other students previously underserved by higher education (Collison, 1998; Ruch, 2001; Sperling and Tucker, 1997).

Proprietary schools have created a niche for themselves through purposeful targeting and aggressive recruitment of women and students of color (Ruch, 2001). Close to half of those attending proprietary schools, such as DeVry Institute and the University of Phoenix, are students of color or first-generation students (Ruch, 2001; Sperling and Tucker, 1997). According to Collison (1998), several proprietary institutions are among the top one hundred institutions graduating African American and women students in business, computer science, and engineering. Proprietary institutions often are considered more flexible, cost-effective, and less selective than not-for-profit colleges and universities, and are also desirable because of their reputation for first-rate job placement for graduates.

Single-Sex Education: Women's Colleges. All women, regardless of race, were educationally disadvantaged prior to the Civil War, because of societal norms which dictated that only white men should receive formal postsecondary education. Colleges for women were founded to remedy this situation. The founding of these institutions was largely to benefit white women, since African American women were neither sufficiently wealthy to attend college nor considered intellectually capable in general (Lerner, 1992, 1993). One exception was Spellman College, which was established to serve black women.

Today, there are eighty-two women's colleges in twenty-five states. They include both private and public, two-year and four-year, and predominantly white and historically black institutions (Sebrechts, 2001). Many women's colleges have religious affiliations. Despite the historic context in which they were established, women's colleges are considered by many to be relevant today because gender bias still is evident in American educational institutions (Aragon and Zamani, 2002; Hagg, 2001; Lomotey, 1997).

Although single-sex institutions are thought by some to produce higher achievement levels among women than do coeducational colleges and universities, socioeconomic class benefits also have been attached to those attending private women's colleges, particularly those that are most selective (Hagg, 2001). It was not until the 1960s that the most elite women's colleges (for example, the "Seven Sisters," including Wellesley, Vassar, Bryn Mawr, and Barnard) actively recruited African American women (Perkins, 1997). Once recruited, they found success similar to that of their white counterparts. For example, Perkins (1997) stated that African American graduates of women's colleges in the mid-1960s are among the "who's who" of black American elites. According to *Black Enterprise* magazine in 1991 (cited in Sebrechts, 2001), four of the twenty most powerful African American women in corporate America were alumnae of women's colleges. Like coeducational HBCUs, women's colleges do a better job of encouraging African American women to major in math or science and are associated with a greater likelihood of producing graduates

14   MEETING THE NEEDS OF AFRICAN AMERICAN WOMEN

that eventually receive doctoral degrees (Hagg, 2001; Sebrechts, 2001; Wolf-Wendel, 1998).

Although there are eighty-two women's colleges, only 2.5 percent of women have attended these institutions over the last three decades (Sebrechts, 2001). There were 252 women's colleges in 1960, but by 1993, well over 60 percent of them had closed. In 1997, five of the eighty-two remaining women's colleges were two-year institutions (Wolf-Wendel and Pedigo, 1999).

At the core of colleges designed for special populations are opportunities for African American women to achieve self-actualization in ways that are often not available in other educational contexts. Many institutions of higher education have successfully met the needs of African American women, but research distinguishes special populations colleges—such as coeducational HBCUs, historically black women's colleges, and women's colleges—as having the most positive and profound impact on the lives of African American women (Bowman, 1992; Drewry and Doermann, 2001; Gray, 2001; Wolf-Wendel, 1998; Wolf-Wendel, Blacker, and Morphew, 2000).

Among the many strengths of HBCUs and single-sex institutions are their culturally based educational efforts that promote their missions to provide opportunities for academic and social growth, leadership development, and matriculation to degree completion. African American women attending HBCUs report greater cultural congruity (fit between their educational needs and resources in the environment) and life satisfaction than do those enrolled at PWIs (Constantine and Watt, 2002). Although African American women students perceive less racial bias at HBCUs than at PWIs, they also find gender discrimination in existence at HBCUs (Bonner, 2001; Bowman, 1995; Fleming, 1996).

Fostering the Growth of African American Women: Implications for Practice

Programs and approaches to meeting the needs of African American women are addressed in the chapters that follow, but research at HBCUs and women's colleges provides several suggestions appropriate for coeducational or predominantly white institutions:

- Create a substantive African American presence at majority institutions through a firm commitment to attracting African American students, faculty, and staff irrespective of the retrenchment on affirmative action in higher education, in order to reduce feelings of marginalization among African American women.
- Develop and maintain programs and policies that attend to the special concerns and needs of African American women on campus.
- Allocate financial and human resources to support institutional efforts that seek to address racial and gender bias.

- Augment curriculum and classroom experiences in order to be more inclusive of African American women and to foster their academic development, particularly in white male–dominated disciplines.

References

Altbach, P. G., Lomotey, K., and Rivers, S. "Race in Higher Education: The Continuing Crisis." In W. A. Smith, P. G. Altbach, and K. Lomotey (eds.), *The Racial Crisis in American Higher Education: Continuing Challenges for the Twenty-First Century.* Albany: State University of New York Press, 2002.

Aragon, S. R., and Zamani, E. M. "Promoting Access and Equity Through Minority-Serving Institutions." In *Readings on Equal Education,* Vol. 18: *Equity and Access in Higher Education: New Perspectives for the New Millennium* (M. C. Brown and K. Freeman, eds.). New York: AMS Press, 2002.

Bennett, L., Jr. *Before the Mayflower: A History of Black America.* (6th ed.) New York: Penguin Books, 1998.

Billingsley, A. *Climbing Jacob's Ladder: The Enduring Legacy of African American Families.* New York: Simon & Schuster, 1992.

Bonner, F. B. "Addressing Gender Issues in the Historically Black College and University Community: A Challenge and Call to Action." *Journal of Negro Education,* 2001, *70*(3), 176–191.

Bowman, J. W. *America's Black Colleges: The Comprehensive Guide to Historically and Predominantly Black Four-Year Colleges and Universities.* Pasadena, Calif.: Sandcastle Publishing, 1992.

Bowman, S. L. "African American or Female: How Do We Identify Ourselves?" Paper presented at the annual meeting of the American Psychological Association, New York, Aug. 1995. (ED 409 384)

Brint, S., and Karabel, J. *The Diverted Dream: Community Colleges and the Promise of Educational Opportunity in America, 1900–1985.* New York: Oxford University Press, 1989.

Brown, M. C., II, and Davis, J. E. "The Historically Black College as Social Contract, Social Capital, and Social Equalizer." *Peabody Journal of Education,* 2001, *76,* 31–49.

Carter, D. F. "The Impact of Institutional Choice and Environments on African American and White Students' Degree Expectations." *Research in Higher Education,* 1999, *40,* 17–41.

Carter, D. F. *A Dream Deferred? Examining the Degree Aspirations of African American and White College Students.* New York: Routledge Falmer, 2001.

Chafe, W. H., Gavins, R., and Korstad, R. *Remembering Jim Crow: African Americans Tell About Life in the Segregated South.* New York: New Press, 2001.

Chenoweth, K. "Forthcoming ETS Report Proclaims the Importance of HBCUs." *Black Issues in Higher Education,* 1997, *14,* 16–19.

Clayton, R. *Some Characteristics of the Historically Black Colleges.* 1979. (ED 176 651)

Cohen, A. M. *The Shaping of American Higher Education: Emergence and Growth of the Contemporary System.* San Francisco: Jossey-Bass, 1998.

Cohen, A., and Brawer, F. *The American Community College.* (4th ed.) San Francisco: Jossey-Bass, 2003.

Collison, M.N.K. "Proprietary Preference." *Black Issues in Higher Education,* 1998, *15*(10), 31–32.

Constantine, M. G., and Watt, S. K. "Cultural Congruity, Womanist Identity Attitudes, and Life Satisfaction Among African American College Women Attending Historically Black and Predominantly White Institutions." *Journal of College Student Development,* 2002, *43*(2), 184–194.

Cross, T., and Slater, R. B. "The Troublesome Decline in African-American College Student Graduation Rates." *Journal of Blacks in Higher Education,* 2001, *33,* 102–109.

Dougherty, K. J. *The Contradictory College: The Conflicting Origins, Impacts, and Future of the Community College.* New York: State University of New York, 1994.

Drewry, H. N., and Doermann, H. *Stand and Prosper: Private Black Colleges and Their Students.* Princeton, N.J.: Princeton University Press, 2001.

Fleming, J. "Black Women in Black and White College Environments: The Making of a Matriarch." In C. Turner, M. Garcia, A. Nora, and L. I. Rendon (eds.), *Racial and Ethnic Diversity in Higher Education.* San Francisco: Jossey-Bass, 1996.

Giddings, P. *When and Where I Enter: The Impact of Black Women on Race and Sex in America.* New York: Morrow, 1984.

Grandy, J. "Persistence in Science of High-Ability Minority Students: Results of a Longitudinal Study. *Journal of Higher Education,* 1998, 69(6), 589–620.

Gray, W. H., III. "The Case for All-Black Colleges." *ERIC Review: The Path to College.* Nov. 2001, 5(3). [http://www.eric.ed.gov/resources/ericreview/vol5no3/black.html]. Retrieved Dec. 22, 2002.

Gregory, S. T. *Black Women in the Academy: The Secrets to Success and Achievement.* (2nd ed.) Lanham, Md.: University Press of America, 1999.

Guyden, J. A. "Two-Year Historically Black Colleges." In B. K. Townsend (ed.), *Two-Year Colleges for Women and Minorities: Enabling Access to the Baccalaureate.* New York: Falmer Press, 1999.

Hagg, P. "Women and the Path to College." *ERIC Review: The Path to College,* Nov. 2001, 5(3). [http://www.eric.ed.gov/resources/ericreview/vol5no3/women.html]. Retrieved Dec. 22, 2002.

Hayes, E. "Creating Knowledge About Women's Learning." In E. Hayes, D. D. Flannery, and Associates, *Women as Learners: The Significance of Gender in Adult Learning.* San Francisco: Jossey-Bass, 2000a.

Hayes, E. "Social Contexts." In E. Hayes, D. D. Flannery, and Associates, *Women as Learners: The Significance of Gender in Adult Learning.* San Francisco: Jossey-Bass, 2000b.

Historically Black Colleges and Universities Fact Book, Vol. 1: *Junior and Community Colleges.* Washington, D.C.: Division of Black American Affairs, U.S. Department of Education, 1983.

Hobbs, F., and Stoops, N. "Demographic Trends in the 20th Century: Census 2000 Special Reports." Washington, D.C.: U.S. Department of Commerce.

Hope, R. O. "Revitalizing Minority Colleges and Universities." In L. I. Rendón & R. O. Hope (eds.), *Educating a New Majority: Transforming America's Educational System for Diversity.* San Francisco: Jossey-Bass, 1996.

Hurtado, S., Milem, J. F., and Clayton-Pedersen, A. *Enacting Diverse Learning Environments: Improving the Climate for Racial/Ethnic Diversity in Higher Education.* ASHE-ERIC Higher Education Report, 26(8), 1999.

Jackson, K. W., and Swan, L. A. "Institutional and Individual Factors Affecting Black Undergraduate Student Performance: Campus Race and Student Gender." In W. R. Allen, E. G. Epps, and N. Z. Haniff (eds.), *College in Black and White: African American Students in Predominantly White and Historically Black Public Universities.* Albany: State University of New York Press, 1991.

Jackson, L. R. "The Influence of Both Race and Gender on the Experiences of African American College Women." *Review of Higher Education,* 1998, 21(4), 359–375.

Joiner, L. L. "Success to the Third Degree." *Black Issues in Higher Education,* 2001, 18(11), 42–43.

Julia, M. *Constructing Gender: Multicultural Perspectives in Working with Women.* Belmont, Calif.: Brooks/Cole Thomas Learning, 2000.

Lerner, G. *Black Women in White America: A Documentary History.* New York: Vintage Books, 1992.

Lerner, G. *The Creation of Feminist Consciousness: From the Middle Ages to 1870.* New York: Oxford University Press, 1993.

Lomotey, K. "Introduction." In K. Lomotey (ed.), *Sailing Against the Wind: African Americans and Women in U.S. Education.* Albany: State University of New York Press, 1997.

Malveaux, J. "Despite Education, Black Workers Still Face Challenges." *Black Issues in Higher Education,* 1998, *15*(16), 28.

Malveaux, J. "The Campus Gender Gap: A Women's Issue." *Black Issues in Higher Education,* 2002, *19*(2), 38.

Moses, Y. T. *Black Women in Academe: Issues and Strategies.* Washington, D.C.: Project on the Status and Education of Women, Association of American Colleges, 1989.

National Center for Education Statistics. *The Condition of Education 2002.* Washington, D.C.: Office of Educational Research and Improvement, U.S. Department of Education, 2002.

Ogbu, J. U. "Literacy and Schooling in Subordinated Cultures: The Case of Black Americans." In K. Lomotey (ed.), *Going to School: The African American Experience.* Albany: State University of New York Press, 1990.

"The Ominous Gender Gap in African American Higher Education." *Journal of Blacks in Higher Education,* 1999, *23,* 6–9.

Pascarella, E. T., and others. "Does Community College Attendance Versus Four-Year College Attendance Influence Students' Educational Plans?" *Journal of College Student Development,* 1998, *39*(2), 179–193.

Peeke, G. *Mission and Change: Institutional Mission and Its Application to the Management of Further and Higher Education.* Bristol, Pa.: Society for Research into Higher Education and Open University Press, 1994.

Perkins, L. M. "The African American Female Elite: The Early History of African American Women in the Seven Sister Colleges, 1880–1960." *Harvard Educational Review,* 1997, *67*(4), 718–756.

Phillippe, K., and Patton, M. *National Profile of Community Colleges: Trends and Statistics.* (3rd ed.) Washington, D.C.: Community College Press, 2000.

Pincus, F., and Archer, E. *Bridges to Opportunity: Are Community Colleges Meeting the Transfer Needs of Minority Students?* New York: Academy for Educational Development and College Entrance Examination Board, 1989.

Renner, K. E. "Racial Equity and Higher Education." *Academe,* Jan.–Feb. 2003, pp. 38–43.

Ruch, R. S. *Higher Ed, Inc.: The Rise of the For-Profit University.* Baltimore, Md.: Johns Hopkins University Press, 2001.

Ruffins, P. "Patterson Research Institute Reports on Educational Profile of African Americans." *Black Issues in Higher Education,* 1997, *14,* 14–17.

Sebrechts, J. S. "Women's Colleges: A Legacy of High-Achieving Women." *ERIC Review: The Path to College,* Nov. 2001. [http://www.eric.ed.gov/resources/ericreview/vol5no3/highach.html]. Retrieved Dec. 22, 2002.

Sinton, R. S. "The Influence of Context and Reference Group Orientation on the First-Semester Experiences of Undergraduate Women at a Predominantly White Research University." Unpublished doctoral dissertation, The Pennsylvania State University, 1996.

Sperling, J., and Tucker, R. W. *For-Profit Higher Education: Developing a World Class Workforce.* New Brunswick, N.J.: Transaction Publishers and Rutgers, The State University of New Jersey, 1997.

Townsend, B. K. *Two-Year Colleges for Women and Minorities: Enabling Access to the Baccalaureate.* New York: Falmer Press, 1999.

Trent, W. T. "Focus on Equity: Race and Gender Differences in Degree Attainment, 1975–76; 1980–81." In W. R. Allen, E. G. Epps, and N. Z. Haniff (eds.), *College in Black and White: African American Students in Predominantly White and Historically Black Public Universities.* Albany: State University of New York Press, 1991.

"The Troublesome Decline in African American College Student Graduation Rates." *Journal of Blacks in Higher Education,* 2001, *33,* 102–109.

Turner, M. R. "Don't Forget the Women." *Black Issues in Higher Education,* 2001, *18*(6), 34.

University of Michigan. "U.S. Supreme Court Agrees to Hear Admissions Lawsuits." [http://www.umich.edu/~newsinfo/Releases/2002/Dec02/r120202.html]. Dec. 2, 2002. Retrieved Dec. 10, 2002.

U.S. Department of Education. "College Enrollment by Racial and Ethnic Group, Selected Years, 1999." [http://www.ed.gov]. Retrieved Aug. 30, 2002.

Wagener, U., and Nettles, M. T. "It Takes a Community to Educate Students." *Change,* 1998, *30*(2), 18–25.

White, J. *Adult Women in Community Colleges: ERIC Digest.* Los Angeles: ERIC Clearinghouse for Community Colleges, 2001. (ED 451 860)

Wolf-Wendel, L. "Models of Excellence: The Baccalaureate Origins of Successful European American Women, African American Women, and Latinas." *Journal of Higher Education,* 1998, *69,* 141–186.

Wolf-Wendel, L., Blacker, B. D., and Morphew, C. C. "Dollars and Sense: Institutional Resources and the Baccalaureate Origins of Women Doctorates." *Journal of Higher Education,* 2000, *71,* 165–186.

Wolf-Wendel, L., and Pedigo, S. "Two-Year Women's Colleges: Silenced, Fading, and Almost Forgotten." In B. K. Townsend (ed.), *Two-Year Colleges for Women And Minorities: Enabling Access to the Baccalaureate.* New York: Falmer Press, 1999.

Zamani, E. M., and Brown, M. C. "Affirmative Action in Postsecondary Educational Settings: The Historic Nexus of Meritocracy and Access." *Higher Education Policy,* 2003, *16,* 27–38.

EBONI M. ZAMANI is assistant professor of higher education administration at Eastern Michigan University in Ypsilanti, Michigan.

2

Applying appropriate theoretical frameworks for black women is challenging because many theories are very general and do not consider multiple identities and roles. Critical race theory and black feminist thought are suggested as appropriate frameworks and applied to the needs of black women in higher education.

Theoretical Frameworks for African American Women

Mary F. Howard-Hamilton

Finding and applying theoretical constructs that are appropriate for explaining and understanding the experiences of African American women can be challenging. Traditional theories used in student affairs practice, for example, are very general and so might miss important issues encountered or attributes embodied by African American women.

Understanding why the experiences of African American women are different from those of other women and those of African American men is steeped in the historical progression and ideology of black people in the United States. In the early nineteenth century, African American women were viewed not as being financial contributors to the household but as being supportive of their spouses and dealing with domestic duties (Guy-Sheftall and Bell-Scott, 1989; Payton, 1985). Educational attainment was not intended for persons (particularly black women) who were considered to be less than human, slaves or not. During this time, blacks were concerned with uplifting their race—men and women—and thus were not focused on gender issues.

However, the egalitarian attitudes of black men diminished during the period following the Emancipation Proclamation. An influx of black men was educated after the Emancipation Proclamation in all academic disciplines; conversely, the women who did manage to attend college primarily became elementary and secondary school teachers. Double oppression—racism and sexism—was born for African American women when their subordinate status was assumed and enforced by white and black men as well as white women.

Female educators—for example Lucy Slowe, Howard University's dean of students in the late 1930s—found that black women faced multiple challenges when entering college. First, they had little experience in public or community affairs; second, they had internalized traditional beliefs about women's roles due to gender-bound upbringing; and third, they had adopted a self-defeating perspective on life (Slowe, cited in Guy-Sheftall and Bell-Scott, 1989). One can argue that very little has changed for African American women in higher education over the past two centuries. Stereotypes and inequities continue to exist and create formidable roadblocks for them as they attempt to gain educational and economic parity in this society.

Overall, the development and socialization of African American women have been molded and understood within the framework of perceptions and agendas of members of the dominant society. Selecting appropriate theories for understanding the needs of African American women should, however, be based on their cultural, personal, and social contexts, which clearly differ significantly from those of men and women who have not experienced racial and gender oppression. In the words of Carroll (1982), "the Black woman in higher education faces greater risks and problems now than in the past" because she is in a place previously occupied by the dominant group, and the numbers are growing on college campuses—she is becoming more "visible" (p. 115); it is up to faculty and administrators to ameliorate these issues. In this chapter, two theoretical frameworks are presented that delineate factors crucial to developing insight into the developmental and societal issues faced by African American women.

Student Development Theories

Long-established student development theories have been the guiding paradigms for working with college students for over forty years (Howard-Hamilton, 1997). "Institutions have embraced and adopted theories developed by Chickering, Perry, Kohlberg, Holland, Super, Loevinger, and Sanford" (Howard-Hamilton, 1997, p. 18).

Within the past two decades, new theories or models have been created, researched, and published that have included the voices of women (Baxter Magolda, 1992, 1999; King and Kitchener, 1994), people of color (Wijeyesinghe and Jackson, 2001), and other groups who have been marginalized or oppressed (Torres, 1999; Torres and Phelps, 1997; Hardiman and Jackson, 1997). Valuing the cultural differences that students bring to our college campuses is important for their personal growth and development. However, the use of a single lens or perspective, even one including a "melting pot" view of diversity, cannot help all students, particularly African American women, to feel secure about immersing themselves in the university environment When black women do not see themselves represented within the institutional structure or classroom environment and all students seem to be treated from a "one size fits all" frame of reference, there is a loss of individualism as well as gender and cultural constructs. A strong ego and racial ethnic identity does not allow for self-blame and instead builds a strong black feminist ethic grounded in the belief that the personal is political and that social structures and systems can cause personal dysfunction.

Two of the theoretical frameworks that offer promise for understanding the intersecting identities of African American women and explaining ways in which their needs can be addressed effectively are black feminist thought and critical race theory.

Black Feminist Thought

Collins's (1990, 1998, 2002) discussion of black feminist thought suggests that marginal positions in academic settings have been occupied by African American women for an extended period. This marginality is viewed as the "outsider within" status, in which black women have been invited into places where the dominant group has assembled, but they remain outsiders because they are still invisible and have no voice when dialogue commences. A sense of belonging can never exist because there is no personal or cultural fit between the experiences of African American women and the dominant group. Since there is no place, space, or stance provided for this cohort, Collins's paradigm posits the importance of ideas "produced by Black women that clarify a standpoint of and for Black women" (Collins, 2002, p. 468).

There are three key themes in black feminist thought (Collins, 2002). First, the framework is shaped and produced by the experiences black women have encountered in their lives, even though others have documented their stories. Second, although the stories and experiences of each woman are unique, there are intersections of experiences between and among black women. Third, although commonalities do exist among black women, the diversity of class, religion, age, and sexual orientation of black women as a group are multiple contexts from which their experiences can be revealed and understood. These themes may not become apparent to African American women initially, so one role of "Black female intellectuals is to produce facts and theories about the Black female experience that will clarify a Black woman's standpoint for Black women" (Collins, 2002, p. 469).

Further delineation of the themes of black feminist thought provides greater insight into the paradigm and how the concepts were formed. The first theme implies that many people besides African American women have shaped their identity. The theme also implies that the ways in which others have shaped black women's identity have been erroneous and stereotypical. These "externally defined images have been designed to control assertive Black female behavior" (Collins, 2002, p. 469). Therefore, it is important that self-valuation, self-definition, and knowledge validation replace the negative images of self in the minds of these women. Oppressive images are difficult to erase, however, when they been reinforced over a long period.

The multiple identities of race, gender, and class are interlocking components of most African American women's identities. Furthermore, these multifaceted identities are immersed in oppression and subordinate their "status in an array of either/or dualities" (Collins, 2002, p. 472). Placement at the inferior end of the status continuum because of these dualities has been the pivotal reason for the perpetual domination of black women.

The lives of African American women have been shaped by so many outside influences that the third theme encourages them to develop, redefine, and explain their own stories based on the importance of black women's culture. These new stories have come in song, dance, literature, film, and other media, helping to share the culture and experiences of black women from their own personal points of view. The philosophy of black feminist thought has not been entertained by many women of color because they do not view themselves as feminists based on the mainstream definition. But Collins's perspectives certainly provide a deeper context and meaning for African American women who have been searching for a voice within rather than one heard from the outside.

Critical Race Theory

Critical race theory (CRT) is a theoretical framework that was generated by scholars of color who study law and legal policies and who are concerned about racial subjugation in society (Delgado and Stefancic, 2001; Smith, Altbach, and Lomotey, 2002; Villalpando and Bernal, 2002). Research by these scholars revealed that persons in power designed laws and policies that were supposed to be race-neutral but still perpetuated racial and ethnic oppression. "This framework emphasizes the importance of viewing policies and policy making in the proper historical and cultural context to deconstruct their racialized content" (Villalpando and Bernal, 2002, pp. 244–245). According to critical race theorists, ideas such as color blindness and meritocracy systematically disadvantage people of color and further advantage whites. Avoiding the issue of race allows individuals to "redress only extremely egregious racial harms, ones that everyone should notice and condemn" (Delgado and Stefancic, 2001, p. 22). Thus, other types of covert racial atrocities are avoided, neglected, and excused. There should be an overt color-conscious effort to reduce racist acts in our society.

- Recognizes that racism is endemic to American life
- Expresses skepticism toward dominant claims of neutrality, objectivity, color blindness, and meritocracy
- Challenges ahistoricism and insists on a contextual and historical analysis of institutional policies

- Insists on recognizing the experiential knowledge of people of color and our communities of origin in analyzing society
- Is interdisciplinary and crosses epistemological and methodological boundaries
- Works toward eliminating racial oppression as part of the broader goal of ending all forms of oppression (Villalpando and Bernal, 2002, p. 245)

Critical race theory as applied to education differs slightly from its legal applications "because it attempts to foreground race and racism in the research as well as challenge the traditional paradigms, methods, texts, and separate discourse on race, gender, and class by showing how these social constructs intersect to impact on communities of color" (Solorzano, Ceja, and Yosso, 2000, p. 63). Moreover, there is a focus on a liberating and transformative experience for persons of color by exploring multiple cultural and personal contexts that make up their identity, such as race, gender, class, and socioeconomic status. The origins of racial oppression are explored in ethnic studies, women's studies, law, psychology, sociology, and history, then discourse is established so that the common themes and threads can be shared.

Methods used to awaken the consciousness of disadvantaged groups are exposure to microaggressions, creation of counterstories, and development of counterspaces. Conscious, unconscious, verbal, nonverbal, and visual forms of insults directed toward people of color are called microaggressions (Delgado and Stefancic, 2001; Solorzano, Ceja, and Yosso, 2000). These diatribes are pervasive, often covert, innocuous, and nebulous and thus are difficult to investigate. This causes tremendous anxiety for those who experience this racist psychological battering.

Critical race theory uses counterstories in the form of discussion, archives, and personal testimonies because it acknowledges that some members of marginalized groups, by virtue of their marginal status, tell previously untold or different stories based on experiences that challenge the discourse and beliefs of the dominant group (Delgado and Stefancic, 2001; Villalpando and Bernal, 2002). Counterstorytelling is used to cast doubt on existing ideas or myths held by majority group members. A safe place and space, known as a counterspace, should be provided when marginalized groups share their counterstories.

Students of color establish academic and social counterspaces on campus by finding people who look like themselves and establishing a space that is comfortable and hospitable for them (Solorzano, Ceja, and Yosso, 2000). These counterspaces may be in a physical structure such as a cultural center, or may be simply the presence of participants in an organization that espouses Africentric values such as a black fraternity or sorority, or a study group. The primary emphasis of the counterspace is on finding shelter from the daily torrent of microaggressions and to be in a place that is validating and supportive. "When the ideology of racism is examined and racist injuries are named, victims of racism can find their voice. Further, those injured by racism discover that they are not alone in their marginality. They become empowered participants, hearing their own stories of others, listening to how the arguments are framed, and learning to make the arguments themselves" (Solorzano, Ceja, and Yosso, 2000, p. 64).

Theory to Practice

These theories address the plights faced by African American women, specifically racism, sexism, classism, loneliness, microaggressions, marginality syndrome, and the status of outsider within (Collins, 1990, 1998, 2002; Robinson and Howard-Hamilton, 2000). One must ask, then, how African American women can address these challenges during college. In the following paragraphs, I offer some suggestions for persons who work with African American women and for the women themselves. Individuals such as black men, other people of color, or people from differing religions or sexual orientations who have experienced the outsider-within syndrome also may benefit from the lessons on how to become empowered, identifying one's own cultural context, and renaming history.

Faculty and administrators should maintain a concerted effort to provide course materials and programming that are relevant to African American women. In the classroom, counteracting the outsider-within syndrome can be accomplished by selecting course materials and designing assignments that allow students the flexibility and freedom to find themselves in the canon. This book, for example, is written in a form of black feminist thought because the researchers have decided to move black women's voices to the center of attention and analysis (Collins, 2002).

Faculty who teach from an inclusive feminist framework should also design classroom experiences to facilitate continual dialogue, assign journal writing so that students can create counterstories, engage in creative projects that are group-oriented, and encourage opportunities to shift environments and move outside of one's comfort zone.

Evaluation of student projects is important to efforts to recreate or improve on the assignments in the future. "Post-assessments, summary papers, student-faculty conferences, and teaching-evaluation instruments are ways to obtain information on the effectiveness of the assignments and strategies used in class and their impact upon students' learning and lives" (Dawson-Threat, 1997, p. 37). Collins (2002) does warn facilitators of this process that helping students recognize the outsider-within mindset "is bound to generate tension, for people who become outsiders within are forever changed by their new status" (p. 480). Therein lies the reason that this must be a joint curricular-cocurricular endeavor: when students come to the realization that they have been viewed as peripheral participants by others, they may become angry and unsure about how they are to gain the respect of others once they move into the inner circle of the conversations.

The facilitor should continue to educate the student about the new status and how to manage the continual tension that arises when one's consciousness has been raised.

When the reawakening process begins for black women, it is often helpful to refer them to the campus counseling center or cultural center. In these places, a black woman can connect with a person or persons who can support and validate the microaggressions or other insidious forms of racism and sexism she has identified.

More information on counseling, programming, and mentoring is given in following chapters, but one example deserves attention here. The "Waiting to Exhale" retreat at Indiana University has been tremendously successful. The retreat brought African American and white women together to share their stories, similarities, and differences. The program was an overnight activity held at a sorority house on campus, and more than sixty women participated. The retreat facilitator was a member of a black sorority on campus, and she enlisted other organizations and administrators to lead get-acquainted activities; group discussions about male-female relationships and coping and survival strategies; and goal setting to bridge the gap between white women and women of color on campus. Feminist thought and critical race theory intersect in the description of this program: counterstories were developed, a common space was discovered and shared, and the outsider-within status was clearly named and addressed when all voices were heard. All of the participants saw a new way to become united in their struggle against oppression.

Racial microaggressions that occur within academic and social spaces have been studied by Solorzano, Ceja, and Yosso (2000). The researchers found microaggressions have a direct impact on the academic and social lives of students, which in turn lead to the formation of academic and social common spaces and counterspaces. "These counter-spaces serve as sites where deficit notions of people of color can be challenged and where a positive collegiate racial climate can be established and maintained" (Solorzano, Ceja, and Yosso, 2000, p. 70). The researchers also found that African American students create academic and social racial or gender counterspaces in response to their marginality on campus. Specifically, "in separating themselves from racially or gender-uncomfortable situations, this group of African American college students appeared to be utilizing their counter-spaces on their own terms" (Solorzano, Ceja, and Yosso, 2000, p. 71).

In other words, survival for black women is contingent on their ability to find a place to describe their experiences among persons like themselves. Thus, the university community should be prepared to support African American women when they seek a safe haven within predominantly black student associations, black sororities, and black female support groups. Faculty and administrators must be comfortable with black women establishing these spaces, or a vicious oppressive cycle in which the dominant group maintains the status quo on campus and all others remain outsiders within will persist.

Summary

Throughout this monograph, the authors agree unequivocally that "there is no more isolated subgroup in academe than Black women. They have neither race nor sex in common with White males who dominate the decision making stratum of academe; Black males in academe at least share with the White males their predominance over women" (Carroll, 1982, p. 118). Although this quote is over two decades old, it illuminates for the reader that even though we see the world changing, a traditional state of mind still prevails. The African American woman "has been called upon to create herself without model or precedent" (Carroll, 1982, p. 126). The information in this chapter paves the way for a framework that highlights the benefits and support systems for black women that can be created on college and university campuses. Using a theory-to-practice approach integrated with traditional student affairs theories, black feminist thought, and critical race frameworks should allow higher education faculty and staff to enhance the chances for career, academic, personal, and professional success for African American women.

References

Baxter Magolda, M. B. *Knowing and Reasoning in College: Gender-Related Patterns in Students' Intellectual Development.* San Francisco: Jossey-Bass, 1992.

Baxter Magolda, M. B. *Creating Contexts for Learning and Self-Authorship: Constructive-Developmental Pedagogy.* Nashville, Tenn.: Vanderbilt University Press, 1999.

Carroll, C. M. "Three's a Crowd: The Dilemma of the Black Woman in Higher Education." In G. T. Hull, P. B. Scott, and B. Smith (eds.), *All the Women Are White, All the Blacks Are Men, But Some of Us Are Brave: Black Women's Studies.* New York: Feminist Press, 1982.

Collins, P. H. *Black Feminist Thought: Knowledge, Consciousness, and the Politics of Empowerment.* Boston: Unwin Hyman, 1990.

Collins, P. H. *Fighting Words: Black Women and the Search for Justice.* Minneapolis: University of Minnesota Press, 1998.

Collins, P. H. "Learning from the Outsider Within: The Sociological Significance of Black Feminist Thought." In C. S. Turner, A. L. Antonio, M. Garcia, B. V. Laden, A. Nora, and C. Presley (eds.), *Racial and Ethnic Diversity in Higher Education.* Boston: Pearson Custom Publishing, 2002.

Dawson-Threat, J. "Enhancing In-Class Academic Experiences for African American Men." In M. Cuyjet (ed.), *Helping African American Men Succeed in College.* New Directions for Student Services, no. 80. San Francisco: Jossey-Bass, 1997.

Delgado, R., and Stefancic, J. *Critical Race Theory: An Introduction.* New York: New York University Press, 2001.

Guy-Sheftall, B., and Bell-Scott, P. "Finding a Way: Black Women Students and the Academy." In C. S. Pearson, D. L. Shavlik, and J. G. Touchton (eds.), *Educating the Majority: Women Challenge Tradition in Higher Education.* New York: Macmillan, 1989.

Hardiman, R., and Jackson, B. W. "Conceptual Foundation for Social Justice Courses." In M. Adams, L. A. Bell, and P. Griffin (eds.), *Teaching for Diversity and Social Justice: A Sourcebook.* New York: Routledge, 1997.

Howard-Hamilton, M. F. "Theory to Practice: Applying Developmental Theories Relevant to African American Men." In M. Cuyjet (ed.), *Helping African American Men*

Succeed in College. New Directions for Student Services, no. 80. San Francisco: Jossey-Bass, 1997.

King, P. M., and Kitchener, K. S. *Developing Reflective Judgment*. San Francisco: Jossey-Bass, 1994.

Payton, C. R. "Addressing the Special Needs of Minority Women." In N. J. Evans (ed.), *Facilitating the Development of Women*. New Directions for Student Services, no. 29. San Francisco: Jossey-Bass, 1985.

Robinson, T. L., and Howard-Hamilton, M. F. *The Convergence of Race, Ethnicity, and Gender: Multiple Identities in Counseling*. Upper Saddle River, N.J.: Merrill/Prentice Hall, 2000.

Smith, W. A., Altbach, P. G., and Lomotey, K. *The Racial Crisis in American Higher Education: Continuing Challenges for the Twenty-First Century*. New York: State University of New York Press, 2002.

Solorzano, D., Ceja, M., and Yosso, T. "Critical Race Theory, Racial Microaggressions, and Campus Racial Climate: The Experiences of African American College Students." *Journal of Negro Education*, 2000, *69*(1–2), 60–73.

Torres, V. "Validations of a Bicultural Orientation Model for Hispanic College Students." *Journal of College Student Development*, 1999, *40*(3), 285–299.

Torres, V., and Phelps, R. E. "Hispanic American Acculturation and Ethnic Identity: A Bicultural Model." *College Student Affairs Journal*, 1997, *17*(1), 53–68.

Villalpando, O., and Bernal, D. D. "A Critical Race Theory Analysis of Barriers That Impede the Success of Faculty of Color." In W. A. Smith, P. G. Altbach, and K. Lomotey (eds.), *The Racial Crisis in American Higher Education: Continuing Challenges for the Twenty-First Century*. New York: State University of New York Press, 2002.

Wijeyesinghe, C. L., and Jackson, B. W. *New Perspectives on Racial Identity Development: A Theoretical and Practical Anthology*. New York: New York University Press, 2001.

MARY F. HOWARD-HAMILTON *is associate dean of graduate studies and associate professor in the Department of Educational Leadership and Policy Studies, Higher Education and Student Affairs Program, at the W. W. Wright School of Education, Indiana University–Bloomington.*

3

This chapter describes and discusses spiritual lives of African American female college students, including elements of coping, resisting, and developing identity.

Come to the River: Using Spirituality to Cope, Resist, and Develop Identity

Sherry K. Watt

This chapter discusses the role that spirituality plays in the lives of African American college women. The theoretical frameworks of James Fowler, Sharon Parks, and Linda James Myers are viewed through the lens of experiences of African American women in college. Qualitative research results illustrate how African American college women use spiritual understanding to cope, to resist, and to develop their identities. Finally, practical strategies and implications for student affairs professionals are presented.

Introduction

Developing a healthy identity as an African American female is fraught with many challenges. African American college women often turn to spiritual beliefs to cope with the everyday struggles that come with living in a socially and politically oppressive system. For many African American college women, spirituality includes a search for meaning that shapes their identities, which in turn helps them to better cope with the negative messages they receive from society.

African American women often are more easily accepted in mainstream society than their male counterparts, but they still have to maneuver between the larger American society and the smaller African American community, and negotiate living within the latter. Smith (1986) refers to

---

The title of this chapter was inspired by discussions with my Spring 2003 Psychosocial and Identity Development class and adapted from a song by jazz artist Dianne Reeves called "Come to the River."

this as a marginalized position that requires women to navigate at least two cultures. As a consequence, they might not feel they fully belong in either setting. Such an existence can become increasingly more challenging to negotiate, given the acts of racism, sexism, and homophobia that occur daily on college campuses (Hirabayashi, 2000; Hoover, 2001; Smallwood, 2002).

African American college women must pay special attention to redefining the roles that come with pursuing a college education. They must deal with the conflict between what earning a college degree means (higher socioeconomic status, professional advancement) and historical roles (care provider, support for African American men). It is especially taxing on a woman's psychological health to manage these conflicts while trying to overcome negative stereotypical roles imposed by society in order to redefine the self in positive ways. To protect their psychological health and develop identity, African American college women employ an array of strategies to resist negative societal messages.

Research on African American College Women and Spirituality: Coping, Resisting, and Developing Identity

Recognition of increasing racial tension on campuses, low recruitment and retention rates of African American faculty and staff, and challenges of balancing expectations from the larger society and community can lead one to ask how black women can succeed in alienating and unwelcoming environments. Historically, African American women are known for turning to religious and spiritual practices for support (Brown and Gray, 1991; Mattis, 2002).

Most of the research on this topic focuses on spirituality as a coping mechanism (Constantine, Wilton, Gainor, and Lewis, 2002; Thomas, 2001). However, although African American women depend on spiritual guidance to cope, they also employ spirituality as a psychological resistance strategy to deflect negative societal messages (Robinson and Ward, 1991; Robinson and Howard-Hamilton, 1994; Brookins and Robinson, 1995). Researchers also have begun to describe spirituality as an identity construct (Watt, 1997; Stewart, 2002). These three perspectives are described in the following sections.

Spirituality as Coping. Some researchers explore coping styles in the context of the practice of religion (Constantine, Wilton, Gainor, and Lewis, 2002; Eugene, 1995; Mattis, 2002; Thomas, 2001). These researchers speculate that African American women have a wide range of coping strategies (Jackson and Sears, 1992; Mattis, 2002; Thomas, 2001). Howard-Vital (1989) notes that although educated black women have traditionally been important to the African American community, they also feel isolated in their communities and in higher education institutions.

For example, many African American college women find that they are one of a few to leave their community to pursue higher education. Once she arrives on campus it is not unusual for her to be the only woman of color in most of her classes. Thus faculty and other students are not exposed to the experiences of African American women at high rates. Due to their lack of exposure, African American women are often misunderstood and must cope with stereotypes associated with both their race and gender. African American college women might cope positively with this isolation by developing a regimine that includes prayer, bible study, or other rituals that invite the spirit into her daily life, rather than coping negatively by overeating or looking for support in unhealthy relationships. Religious or spiritual rituals may help her to connect with the higher being and her inner strength so she can endure the discomforts associated with pursing higher education. Howard-Vital (1989) emphasized the importance of conducting more research on coping strategies for black women and on the interaction of race and sex in the context of institutions of higher education. She states that this will contribute to understanding what it takes to improve the environmental conditions and ultimately retention rates of African American college women.

Spirituality as Psychological Resistance. The literature examining how African Americans resist negative cultural images is largely conceptual. Robinson and Ward (1991) developed the Resistance Modality Model based on an Africentric worldview, which values the segmentation of spirit and matter (Myers and others, 1991). The Resistance Modality Model acknowledges that African American women can deflect negative attacks from society by using strategies of resistance. The concepts of this model suggest that an Africentric worldview might be psychologically healthy for African Americans (Robinson and Howard-Hamilton, 1994; Robinson and Kennington, 2002; Brookins and Robinson, 1995).

Robinson and Ward (1991) stated that healthy identity development for African American women means employing resistance strategies, yet elsewhere a distinction is made between resistance that is survival-oriented and resistance that is empowering and liberating (Robinson and Howard-Hamilton, 1994). Historically, the African American female image is resilient and strong. The implication is that she is surviving despite the negative influences of society.

Robinson and Ward (1991) point out, however, that resistance just to survive is not enough. Resistance for survival is characterized by "self-denigration due to internalization of negative self images [and] excessive autonomy and individualism at the expense of connectedness to the collective" (Robinson and Howard-Hamilton, 1994, p. 329). For example, an academically gifted African American college woman practicing resistance-for-survival strategies would be concerned that her instructors might perceive her college admission to be a result of an affirmative action quota. Therefore, she would limit public associations with other African Americans so that her image as a scholar would not be tarnished.

If an African American woman is choosing resistance for empowerment and liberation as a strategy, then she will engage in "a self consciousness raising process of seeking to identify and transcend imposed systemic barriers by drawing upon the strengths of [her] history and cultural connections" (Robinson and Howard-Hamilton, 1994, p. 330). For example, an African American college woman engaging in resistance for liberation makes a conscious decision to build a network of African American friends and colleagues in her major, in the community, and even those outside of her race who will send messages to her that counter the negative ones she receives daily from her surroundings. Brookins and Robinson (1995) suggest that learning resistance strategies through rites of passage programs can be a useful approach in preventing behaviors that are characteristic of those living in "an oppressive suboptimal environment" (p. 179).

Spirituality and Developing Identity. Research is beginning to closely examine how faith and spirituality mediate African American college women's development of integrated identities (Stewart, 2002; Watt, 1997). Identity development is one of the primary and most demanding tasks for college students, especially for those who are conscious in their efforts to integrate multiple identities (Chickering and Reisser, 1993). The search for an integrated identity is intense for African American women who exist in a culture where being female and being black are both devalued. Stewart (2002) states that the process of identity development for African American women includes changing definitions of the self from external to internal. Spirituality is central to that process. In a study of African American women, I found that there is a relationship between African American women's self-esteem, racial identity, womanist identity, and faith development (Watt, 1997).

Research that examines how this population copes, psychologically resists, and shapes identity in the face of multiple negative cultural messages establishes that spirituality is central to identity development. A drawback of this research is that it is primarily theoretical and descriptive in nature. Empirical data should be collected to illustrate how African American women develop identity. This will help student affairs practitioners determine how they can successfully make use of spirituality when working with African American college women.

A Framework for African American College Women's Spiritual Identity Development

This section has three purposes. First, it defines faith and spirituality. Second, it assesses the usefulness of the spiritual and faith development work of Fowler and Parks in terms of its fit for understanding experiences of African American college women. Third, it offers a theory by Linda James as a means of understanding African American women's spiritual identity development.

Defining Faith and Spirituality. Many terms have been used to describe the differences between and among faith, religion, and spirituality. Parks and Fowler define faith development as the process of making meaning. Religion generally represents "an institutionalized set of beliefs and practices by which groups and individuals relate to the ultimate" (Burke and others, 1999, p. 252). According to Robinson (2000), "spirituality is internally and experientially defined, transcends the tangible, and connects one to the whole, which includes the universe and all organisms" (p. 163). For the purposes of this chapter, spirituality development is the process one engages in to search for meaning, and this journey may or may not include religious practices.

Theories of Fowler and Parks. The works of Sharon Parks (1986, 2000) and James Fowler (1981) are often used to describe and understand college students' faith or spiritual development. Fowler (1981) describes faith development from a life-span perspective in a six-stage model, whereas Parks's theory specifically focuses on college students and is grounded in student development theory (Love, 2002). Parks (1986) added a stage to Fowler's theory and expanded on the faith development of college students and the impact of the higher education environment on development. Parks (1986, 2000) also differentiates structural and content knowledge. She states that the development of faith is shaped not only by how knowledge is structured but also by the content placed in those structures—for example, particular images, symbols, and ideologies.

Parks's and Fowler's theories are based heavily on the cognitive and moral developmental frameworks of Perry (1970) and Kohlberg (1971). Although Parks's theory considers social and affective dimensions of faith development, its foundation is grounded primarily in the cognitive development framework. In that vein, recent research and writing about spiritual development for student affairs audiences (Love, 2002; Love and Talbot, 1999) use a cognitive developmental perspective to understand faith development while attempting to build a bridge between spirituality and student affairs practice.

Limitations of Applying Parks's and Fowler's Theories to African American College Women's Experience. The aforementioned theories have at least two limitations when used to understand the development of African American college women. The first limitation is these theories' focus on cognitive structuring, neglecting the affective and social domains. One of Parks's basic suppositions about faith development is that "it matters how we think" (2000, p. 53) about ideas, relationships, and community. African American women, however, might be more likely to develop spiritually through feeling than cognition. African Americans are often emotionally expressive and relational (Locke, 1992). Thus, spiritual traditions in the African American community include embracing spirits of ancestors, speaking in tongues, shouting, and feeling the Holy Spirit. These spiritual traditions are ways of experiencing the ultimate that are not dependent on cognition. In fact, cognition might prevent one from receiving the knowledge that comes through feeling. Attempts to understand African American women's spiritual development, then, should give heavier weight to ways of knowing that are not based in cognition.

A second limitation in applying Parks's or Fowler's theories to African American college women's experiences is that there is little reference in those theories to how ethnic culture might influence faith development. Parks (2000) states: "A culture is composed of the forms of life by which a people cultivate and maintain a sense of meaning [and] thus give shape and significance to their experience. . . . Culture mediates a people's faith, ordering, teaching, creating 'how things are' or how life is" (pp. 206–207).

Although Parks (2000) acknowledges that culture mediates faith development, her discussion assumes a collective national or global lens that does not directly acknowledge ethnicity. In contrast, Tisdell (2003) highlights the interdependence of spirituality and culture and states that spirituality is about honoring wholeness and moving toward the authentic self. To move toward wholeness and authenticity, African American women must wrestle with the question "Who am I within a society that devalues my race and gender?" In applying Parks's theory to African American college women's experience, one would need to consider culture on the individual level in addition to interpreting the national or global influences.

Linda James Myers's Theory of Optimal Psychology. It is difficult to find theoretical frameworks that describe the spiritual and identity development process experienced by African American women. This is due, in part, to the limited amount of research about spirituality and identity in this population. At the same time, the abstract nature of constructs of spirituality and identity create challenges for measurement. Nevertheless, Myers and others (1991) have developed a model of identity development that has interpretive value for African American college women. Myers's Optimal Theory Applied to Identity Development (OTAID) model recognizes that "spirituality is an integral part of identity development" (Myers and others, 1991, p. 57).

Myers's (1988) Optimal Theory of Psychology, on which Optimal Theory Applied to Identity Development is based, moves away from the western or Eurocentric historic roots of psychology to take an Africentric view of the world. The basic assumptions of her theory include comparing and contrasting suboptimal (American) and optimal (African) worldviews (Myers and others, 1991). The suboptimal worldview sees spirit and matter as separate. Within this view, self-worth is externally validated, and an individual is left to look for meaning and peace outside herself. In the optimal worldview, spirit and matter are connected and self-worth is intrinsic. The "self . . . is seen as multidimensional[,] encompassing the ancestor, those yet unborn, nature, and community" (Myers, 1988, p. 56). Optimal conditions for life are "yielding peace, joy, harmony, and the increased well-being of the whole" (Myers and others, 1991).

The OTAID model is expressed in six developmental phases (plus a phase zero), beginning with the phase in which an individual is unaware of self and the interconnectedness of life and culminating with the phase in which the individual is fully conscious of self and connectedness to the circle of life (Myers and others, 1991).

In phase zero of the OTAID model, Absence of Conscious Awareness, the individual lacks general awareness and is unable to distinguish between self and environment. In phase one, Individuation, the individual is not separate from his or her family, and identity depends on society's reinforcement. In phase two, Dissonance, the individual begins to have an affective (anger and confusion) response to the negative images from society and has an experience that helps him or her to see that society encompasses a dominant group and a devalued group. This realization begins to affect how the person develops his or her identity. In phase three, Immersion, the individual embraces the devalued parts of his or her identity and begins to have negative feelings about the dominant group while feeling a sense of joy and pride about his or her own devalued parts. In the Internalization stage, phase four, the individual begins to feel a lasting sense of pride and becomes secure in his or her identity. An integrated identity develops, in which the more salient aspects of the self are put into perspective and acknowledged as just one part of the overall identity. In phase five, Integration, the individual exudes a sense of inner security and peace. The individual has a deepened sense of community and begins to have a better understanding of the true nature of oppression. In phase six, Transformation, the individual has reached a definition of self in which he or she understands the interconnectedness of "the ancestors, those yet unborn, nature, and community" (p. 60). The person lives harmoniously, accepting both positive and negative incidents as opportunities for growth.

As previously noted, Myers's theory is based on an Africentric framework (Myers, 1991); therefore, the assumptions underlying the theory have the potential to fit the cultural experiences of African American college women. Myers's theory might be most effective for describing the processes of spiritual and identity development for this population.

Voices of African American College Women

I facilitated four focus-group interviews as part of a larger study of spirituality and identity development (Watt, 1997). The focus groups included forty-eight African American female participants. Analysis of data from the interviews generated seventeen specific and seven overall themes regarding spirituality and identity. In general, the themes demonstrate ways in which the participants' spirituality helped them to cope, psychologically resist, and develop their identity. The themes also revealed ways in which the phases of the OTAID model (Myers and others, 1991) can be applied to the experience of African American college women.

Coping. Analysis of the interviews identified three themes regarding ways that African American college women used spirituality to cope. The first theme, The Challenging College Experience, illustrated how coping with changes in the college environment (for example, leaving home, meeting culturally different people, and returning home) increased their self-knowledge and positively shaped their personal development. The focus group members also discussed coping with disturbing changes in two other themes: Experience of Violence and Meaningfulness of Life. The African American women who shared their stories recalled the violent and unexpected deaths of many peers and the loss of elders to natural causes. These events seemed to emphasize to these women the importance of controlling their own destiny. In response, many of the women coped by adopting spiritual philosophies that helped them to continue with life. For instance, one participant shared her philosophy, "Live each day as if it were your last"; another stated gratefully, "I made it out; not everyone did."

The OTAID model captures how these women moved from Absence of Conscious Awareness in phase zero and worked through the anger and confusion described in phase two, Dissonance. These women described sobering experiences of life transitions and violence that helped them to become more fully aware of the results of living in a society where subtle messages communicate that women and people of color are devalued. These African American women developed philosophies to help them to accept their situations and, at the same time, make meaning of them so that they could persevere.

Psychologically Resisting. African American college women in these focus groups also developed ways to resist negative societal messages. Six themes captured this psychological resistance. The first theme, Symbols, identified symbols and rituals that brought peace and balance. Important symbols included the Christian cross and a sorority crest (representing sisterhood, fellowship, and community service). Essential rituals included reading affirmative books and prayer. The second theme, Education Is Important, revealed the participants' belief that education empowers and creates options. These two themes also provide examples of how the participants internalized messages to help them to rise above their circumstances.

In the remaining four themes, participants expressed ways that they worked toward defining for themselves their relationship with the ultimate. In the theme Visions of God, focus-group members shared evolving visual images of God from a white male image (the historic pictured representation of Jesus Christ) to God as an old black male. Others rejected the idea of a human image and described God as all-knowing, a voice, and a spirit. In the theme Sin, the women described sin as a feeling, an act, or a thought that was not "right" in the spiritual realm. Their understanding of sin appeared to move from being defined by an authority to self-determined definitions that the women used along with their intuition in making personal decisions.

In the themes Mature Faith and Angels in My Midst, focus-group members described interconnectedness with living and deceased ancestors. Mature Faith was described through examples of mothers, aunts, and grandmothers who were perceived to be at higher levels of faith. In the theme Angels in My Midst, many of the respondents shared stories of being watched over by spirits of their ancestors. For example, one woman told how the spirit of her grandmother materialized in front of her as an abusive partner attempted to take her life with a gun. The bullet missed her by inches because she hesitated. These African American college women developed important strategies for psychological resistance. In other words, they learned from the other women in their lives how to define themselves and trust the spiritual aspects of themselves and their lives.

Phase three of the OTAID model, Immersion, encapsulates a psychological resistance strategy. The African American women in these focus groups used symbols and turned to role models to help them make meaning of life as a way of internalizing positive societal messages and rejecting negative ones. Immersion in these positive representations and the embracing of devalued parts of themselves helped these women to survive.

Developing Identity. The process of making meaning helped the African American women in these focus groups shape their identity. Researchers such as Parks (2000) and Gilligan (1982) point out the important role that relationships play in women's development. In the four themes Relationships Are Our Teachers, Strong Women—Absent Men, Responsibility to Younger Siblings/Family, and Important Relationships, the respondents discussed the roles played by different types of relationships in shaping their identity. These themes held stories about how responsible these women felt for paving the way for younger siblings and how relationships with female relatives and fathers (present or absent) were significant in helping them to better understand themselves.

The African American women in these focus groups shaped their identity through life events such as those described in the themes Affirmation and Culture Shock. Milestones such as graduating from high school, becoming a mother, and attending their first day of college signified independence. While in college, encounters with culturally different people raised issues that required these women to think more intently about the question "Who am I?"

Finally, the participants described how one comes to know oneself. Illustrating the Purpose of Life theme, one woman stated that the purpose of life is to "Find out what you are here to learn, find out what you are here to teach, and then act on those things."

The final phases of the OTAID model, Internalization, Integration, and Transformation, accurately characterize the developmental transitions of identity described by the women in these focus groups. As the women searched for answers to the "Who am I" question, they appeared to find the meaning of peace, purpose, and the connectedness between ancestors, the yet unborn, and community.

Implications for Student Affairs Practice

Spirituality development is an important element in African American women's survival strategies. African American women use spirituality in multifaceted ways to cope with difficulty, to resist negative images of themselves, and to develop identity. If student affairs practitioners are knowledgeable in the ways that African American college women depend on spirituality, they may be able to be more intentional and effective in providing support to this population. Student affairs practitioners are essential support for African American college women, and understanding spirituality can only add to their effectiveness. The following strategies are intended to assist student affairs professionals in supporting African American college women's identity development.

1. *Become familiar with suboptimal and optimal coping strategies.* Practitioners need to train their ears to recognize suboptimal and optimal resistance strategies. Avoid supporting the "strong black woman" myth. Listen carefully for the coping mechanisms that these women are using and address them appropriately. Review the Africentric Paradigm constructed by Robinson and Howard-Hamilton (1994), and use it to develop intervention strategies to help African American women.

2. *Prepare programs that speak to the whole person.* Practitioners need to plan programs for African American college women that invite discussion in different developmental domains. Create an environment in which women can discuss what it means to experience life being both female and black. In a society where the dominant discourses devalue women and people of color, it is critical to provide a lot of support for African American college women in developing their identity (Robinson and Watt, 2001).

3. *Provide informed support.* Practitioners need to encourage African American women who are vigorously pursuing self-knowledge on all levels, regardless of the consequences. It is important for helpers to understand that supporting women in this pursuit is a crucial part of the process.

4. *Learn more about your reactions to the cultural experiences of African American women.* It is important that student affairs practitioners engage in the process of becoming multiculturally competent. Evaluate your own beliefs and values, learn more about the educational and societal issues that affect African American women's experience, and intentionally develop interventions that are culturally appropriate and honor the experience of this population (Arredondo, 1999).

5. *Recognize the value of spirituality as both a coping mechanism and a way to optimally resist.* Spirituality development seems to be a central part of African American women's acquisition of self-knowledge. Understanding that this is an important coping mechanism for African American women can expand the ways in which student affairs professionals can provide service to this college population.

References

Arredondo, P., "Multicultural Counseling Competencies as Tools to Address Oppression and Racism." *Journal of Counseling and Development,* 1999, 77(1), 102–109.

Brookins, C. C., and Robinson, T. L. "Rites-of-Passage as Resistance to Oppression." *Western Journal of Black Studies,* 1995, 19(3), 172–179.

Brown, D. R., and Gray, L. E. "Religious Socialization and Educational Attainment Among African Americans: An Empirical Assessment." *Journal of Negro Education,* 1991, 60(3), 411–426.

Burke, M. T., Hackney, H., Hudson, P., Miranti, J., Watts, G. A, and Epp, L. "Spirituality, Religion, and CACREP Curriculum Standards." *Journal of Counseling and Development,* 1999, 77, 251–257.

Chickering, A. W., and Reisser, L. *Education and Identity.* (2nd ed.) San Francisco: Jossey-Bass, 1993.

Constantine, M. G., Wilton, L., Gainor, K. A., and Lewis, E. L. "Religious Participation, Spirituality, and Coping Among African American College Students." *Journal of College Student Development,* 2002, 43(5), 605–613.

Eugene, T. M. "There Is a Balm in Gilead: Black Women and the Black Church as Agents of a Therapeutic Community." *Women and Therapy,* 1995, 16, 55–71.

Fowler, J. *Stages of Faith: The Psychology of Human Development and the Quest for Meaning.* New York: HarperCollins, 1981.

Gilligan, C. *In a Different Voice.* Boston: Harvard University Press, 1982.

Hirabayashi, L. R. "How a Death Threat Became an Opportunity to Connect with My Students." *Chronicle of Higher Education,* May 12, 2000, p. B10.

Hoover, E. "Death Threats and a Sit-In Divide Penn State." *Chronicle of Higher Education,* May 11, 2001, p. A43.

Howard-Vital, M. R. "African American Women in Higher Education: Struggling to Gain Identity." *Journal of Black Studies,* 1989, 20(2), 180–191.

Jackson, A. P., and Sears, S. J. "Implications of an Africentric Worldview in Reducing Stress for African American Women." *Journal of Counseling and Development,* 1992, 71, 184–190.

Kohlberg, L. "Stages of Moral Development." In C. M. Beck, B. S. Crittenden, and E. V. Sullivan (eds.), *Moral Education.* Toronto: University of Toronto Press, 1971.

Locke, D. C. *Increasing Multicultural Understanding: A Comprehensible Model.* Thousand Oaks, Calif.: Sage, 1992.

Love, P. G. "Comparing Spiritual Development and Cognitive Development." *Journal of College Student Development,* 2002, 43(3), 357–373.

Love, P., and Talbot, D. "Defining Spiritual Development: A Missing Consideration for Student Affairs." *NASPA Journal,* 1999, 37(1), 361–375.

Mattis, J. S. "Religion and Spirituality in the Meaning-Making and Coping Experiences of African American Women: A Qualitative Analysis." *Psychology of Women Quarterly,* 2002, 26, 309–321.

Myers, L. J. *Understanding an Afrocentric Worldview: Introduction to an Optimal Psychology.* Dubuque, Iowa: Kendall/Hunt, 1988.

Myers, L. J., Speight, S. L., Highlen, P. S., Cox, C. I., Reynolds, A. L., Adams, E. M., and Hanley, C. P. "Identity Development and Worldview: Toward an Optimal Conceptualization." *Journal of Counseling and Development,* 1991, 70, 54–63.

Parks, S. D. *The Critical Years: Young Adults and the Search for Meaning, Faith, and Commitment.* San Francisco: Harper, 1986.

Parks, S. D. *Big Questions, Worthy Dreams: Mentoring Young Adults in Their Search for Meaning, Purpose, and Faith.* San Francisco: Jossey-Bass, 2000.

Perry, W. G. *Forms of Intellectual and Ethical Development in the College Years: A Scheme.* Austin, Tex.: Holt, Rinehart & Winston, 1970.

Robinson, T. L. "Making the Hurt Go Away: Psychological and Spiritual Healing for African American Women Survivors of Childhood Incest." *Journal of Multicultural Counseling and Development,* 2000, *28,* 160–176.

Robinson, T. L., and Howard-Hamilton, M. "An Afrocentric Paradigm: Foundation for a Healthy Self-Image and Healthy Interpersonal Relationships." *Journal of Mental Health Counseling,* 1994, *16*(3), 327–340.

Robinson, T. L., and Kennington, P.A.D. "Holding Up Half the Sky: Women and Psychological Resistance." *Journal of Humanistic Counseling Education and Development,* 2002, *41,* 164–177.

Robinson, T. L., and Ward, J. V. "'A Belief in Self Far Greater Than Anyone's Disbelief': Cultivating Resistance Among African American Female Adolescents." *Women and Therapy,* 1991, *11*(3/4), 87–104.

Robinson, T. L., and Watt, S. K. "Where No One Goes Begging": Converging Gender, Sexuality, and Religious Diversity in Counseling." In D. C. Locke, J. E. Myers, and E. L. Herr (eds.), *The Handbook of Counseling.* Thousand Oaks, Calif.: Sage, 2001.

Smallwood, S. "Firestorm in Missoula." *Chronicle of Higher Education,* Dec. 6, 2002, p. A12.

Smith, A. "Positive Marginality: The Experience of Black Women as Leaders." In E. Seidman, and J. Rappaport (eds.), *Redefining Social Problems.* New York: Plenum Press, 1986.

Stewart, D. L. "The Role of Faith in the Development of an Integrated Identity: A Qualitative Study of Black Students at a White College." *Journal of College Student Development,* 2002, *43*(4), 579–596.

Thomas, A. J. "African American Women's Spiritual Beliefs: A Guide for Treatment." *Women and Therapy,* 2001, *23*(4), 1–12.

Tisdell, E. J. *Exploring Spirituality and Culture in Adult and Higher Education.* San Francisco: Jossey-Bass, 2003.

Watt, S. K. *Identity and the Making of Meaning: Psychosocial Identity, Racial Identity, Womanist Identity, Self-Esteem, and the Faith Development of African American College Women.* Unpublished doctoral dissertation, North Carolina State University, Raleigh, 1997.

SHERRY K. WATT is assistant professor in the Department of Counseling, Rehabilitation, and Student Development at the University of Iowa in Iowa City.

4

This chapter provides information about personal, academic, and vocational concerns of African American college women and offers culturally relevant counseling frameworks and interventions for working with this population.

Personal, Academic, and Career Counseling of African American Women in College Settings

Madonna G. Constantine, Tawanda M. Greer

African American students account for nearly 8 percent of all college students graduating with bachelor's degrees from U.S. colleges and universities (National Center for Education Statistics, 1998). The majority of African American students in U.S. colleges and universities attend predominantly white institutions (National Center for Education Statistics, 1998). In particular, African American women make up nearly two-thirds of the total number of African Americans attending institutions of higher education, and they represent nearly 13 percent of the total undergraduate enrollment. Because the majority of African American students enrolled in institutions of higher education are African American women, counselors have a professional and ethical obligation to be aware of and knowledgeable about the unique needs of this population.

This chapter is intended to provide information about the myriad personal, academic, and vocational issues of African American college women that are shaped by various cultural factors. In addition, we offer culturally relevant counseling frameworks and interventions for use in working with this population. To illustrate some of these issues, a case example of an African American female college student who is seeking counseling is presented.

Personal Issues of African American College Women

The racial composition of institutions of higher learning shape a variety of personal issues (for example, psychosocial and developmental concerns) for African American female college students (Watson and Kuh, 1996). For instance, in contrast to their white peers, African American women enrolled in predominantly white institutions often experience a lack of support and an unwelcoming academic environment (Schweitzer, Griffin, Ancis, and Thomas, 1999; Trippi and Cheatham, 1989). These women often find themselves on campuses where the level of racial hostility against them from whites in the larger world is also reflected in their collegiate environment. Also, African American women in predominantly white institutions may perceive faculty members, academic supports, and developmental services to be inaccessible (Stage and Hamrick, 1994).

Ancis, Sedlacek, and Mohr (2000) found that African American college students at a predominantly white institution consistently reported more negative racial experiences—such as pressure to conform to negative stereotypes, inequitable treatment by members of the campus community, and faculty racism—compared with their non–African American peers. A qualitative study on the adjustment experiences of African American college students (Schweitzer, Griffin, Ancis, and Thomas, 1999) revealed that their social adjustment could be outlined in terms of four key elements: a sense of underrepresentedness (that is, feeling isolated, overlooked, or misunderstood in the social environment); direct perceptions of racism (that is, personal encounters with racially discriminatory situations, statements, and policies); hesitation, uncertainty, or difficulty in initiating communications with faculty members; and feeling greater comfort with faculty members who were more similar to them in terms of race, sex, department, or field of study.

With regard to African American women's college adjustment, a construct that illustrates how they may perceive the fit between themselves and their academic environment is *cultural congruity* (that is, the level of congruence between individuals' cultural values and the values in the environments in which they function) (Gloria, Robinson Kurpius, Hamilton, and Willson, 1999). Constantine, Robinson, Wilton, and Caldwell (2002) found that black college women reported higher levels of cultural congruity than their black male counterparts. Among African American college women, cultural congruity also has been found to be positively associated with collective self-esteem and social support satisfaction (Constantine, Robinson, Wilton, and Caldwell, 2002), students' decisions to remain in college (Gloria, Robinson Kurpius, Hamilton, and Willson, 1999), and life satisfaction (Constantine and Watt, 2002). Moreover, Constantine and Watt (2002) found that African American women at historically black colleges and universities reported higher levels of cultural congruity and life satisfaction in comparison with African American women at predominantly white institutions. Thus, institutional atmosphere may contribute greatly to the academic, emotional, and social adjustment and personal satisfaction of African American college women.

Some African American women who experience difficulties in adjusting to or dealing with college life may choose to seek personal counseling to address their concerns. Although many writings have discussed a general underuse of mental health and counseling services by college students of color (Constantine, 2002; Sue, Arredondo, and McDavis, 1992), some studies (Boesch and Cimbolic, 1994; Mau and Fernandes, 2001) have suggested that African American students use campus counseling services more frequently than had been previously hypothesized. In addition, June, Curry, and Gear (1990) found that upper-division African American students and African American students who lived close to a college counseling center used mental health services more often than other African American students.

Previous studies have found that African American students who seek counseling tend to present with issues such as financial and academic adjustment concerns (June, Curry, and Gear, 1990), vocational concerns (Mau and Fernandes, 2001), and familial and romantic relational difficulties (Constantine, Chen, and Ceesay, 1997). African American college students who are not in counseling have been found to have greater concerns than their white counterparts about issues such as discomfort in their academic settings, racial discrimination, and lack of career knowledge (Lucas, 1993). African American college women tend to seek counseling services more often than their male peers (Constantine, Chen, and Ceesay, 1997; Tomlinson and Cope, 1988).

An issue that might affect the nature of counseling for African American college women is their expectations about counseling (Constantine and Arorash, 2001). For example, researchers have reported that some African American students may have lower expectations about their counselors' personal commitment to the counseling process than do white students (Kenney, 1994). In fact, African American college women, especially those who are aware of issues such as institutional racism, may view the counseling process itself as a component of a larger oppressive system. As such, African American female college students who expect counselors to be multiculturally competent might encounter practitioners who do not exhibit such competence, thereby deterring them from continuing counseling (Constantine and Arorash, 2001).

Furthermore, African American women may regard college counselors as agents of a system that invalidates them. Because African American women as a group have historically faced racial discrimination and oppression by the dominant culture, they may develop a general wariness of whites that could affect their initial approach and continued experiences in counseling. Such suspicion has been conceptualized as *cultural mistrust,* or the extent to which African Americans mistrust white Americans in certain situations (Terrell and Terrell, 1984). It has been theorized that African Americans who have high levels of cultural mistrust toward whites in their daily life will also exhibit mistrust with a white therapist (Whaley, 2001). In fact, cultural mistrust has been associated with premature termination of counseling among black clients (Terrell and Terrell, 1984).

Among African American college students, high levels of cultural mistrust also have been related to less favorable help-seeking attitudes and expectations about counseling (Nickerson, Helms, and Terrell, 1994) and less frequent self-disclosures with white counselors (Thompson, Worthington, and Atkinson, 1994). Moreover, highly mistrustful African American college women could be suspicious of African American mental health professionals because they may be perceived as assimilated into the dominant white culture (Whaley, 2001).

African American college women who seek psychological counseling may encounter services that do not fit with their own cultural worldviews and, consequently, they may be dissuaded from engaging fully in traditional counseling. Culturally relevant helping frameworks can provide a blueprint for effective personal counseling interventions with African American college women, and the adoption of Africentric worldviews might be especially useful in understanding the experiences of African American college women (Utsey, Adams, and Bolden, 2000). In particular, validating and using components of Africentric worldviews may shape the counseling process to promote positive psychosocial development in African American college women.

Group counseling interventions that reflect Africentric cultural values also have been found to be effective with African American college women (Brown, 1994; Brown, Lipford-Sanders, and Shaw, 1995). In particular, "Kujichagulia" (Brown, Lipford-Sanders, and Shaw, 1995) and "Images of Me" (Brown, 1994) represent examples of group interventions that can empower African American college women as racial beings and motivate them to matriculate successfully on predominantly white campuses. These types of Africentric interventions can validate African American beauty standards for African American women who may have internalized negative images of black women. The interventions may provide safe and accepting places where group members can share their experiences and struggles and support their peers who may be struggling in potentially oppressive school environments. Moreover, the nature of group work may resonate strongly with the African American cultural values of communalism and interdependence.

Academic and Career Issues of African American College Women

In general, students in institutions of higher education are preparing themselves for greater career opportunities. For African American college women, this preparation has specific dimensions related to current social conditions that may inhibit their access to upwardly mobile positions, equitable pay, and bias-free career environments (Murry and Mosidi, 1993). African American women may face intense struggles and challenges within work settings because their professional experiences often take place in the context of racist and sexist environments. African American women already may be encountering such oppression, particularly in predominantly white universities and in math and science disciplines (Hendricks, 1994).

African American female college students may also have limited access to role models of the same race or sex within their fields, which may affect how attainable they perceive their career goals to be (Hendricks, 1994). The realities of the employment market and African American women's lack of exposure to some careers can dictate a measured view of available career options (Bingham and Ward, 2001). Therefore, despite initial motivations for improving their career options and mobility, some African American college women may anticipate having restricted career options resulting from limited access to high-level occupations, the influences of race-based and gender-based stereotypes, and a lack of role models in their desired field. Because of cultural stigmas about engaging in personal counseling and the tangible insidious effects of discrimination in the work world, it may not be surprising that research has shown that African Americans are more likely to seek academic and vocational counseling than personal counseling (June, Curry, and Gear, 1990).

Academic counseling for African American women has been found to improve undergraduate grades (Giles-Gee, 1989; Young and Rogers, 1991) and retention rates in higher education (Trippi and Cheatham, 1989, 1991). For example, Young and Rogers (1991) reported that participants in an academic advising program for first-year African American college students had higher mean grade point averages than nonparticipants. Effective academic counseling outcomes with African American college women may result from establishing a counseling relationship early after their entrance into school, active and concrete resolution of presenting concerns, and maintaining an ongoing counseling relationship that provides long-term developmental activities. For African American college women, academic interventions that are multidimensional (that is, those that address personal, social-historical, and institutional obstacles that affect academic performance) also may help them to develop sufficient coping resources to deal with challenging academic circumstances (Giles-Gee, 1989).

Vocational counselors working with African American college women should use systemic perspectives to assess and understand the relevance of historical, economic, political, educational, social, and familial influences, as well as intrapsychic factors such as racial and ethnic identity, on these women's career development (Bingham and Ward, 2001). Dominant career counseling models, such as trait-factor theories and Super's life-span approach, have been criticized for not accounting for contextual influences in the career development process. Career counseling theories that are inclusive of race-related contextual influences have been presented in the literature (Thomas and Alderfer, 1989), although many are presented without empirical validation. For instance, Bingham and Ward (2001) presented a "culturally appropriate career counseling model" that provided a framework for actively infusing cultural issues into the career counseling process. Their framework addressed the following issues: establishment of a culturally appropriate relationship (for example, acknowledging how counselors' and clients' cultural backgrounds might affect their working alliance); identification of various issues that might affect the career development process (for example, cognitive, social-emotional, environmental, behavioral, and external barriers); assessment of cultural variables in regard to career development (for example, the confluence of race, ethnicity, sex, family, and the dominant group on career development issues); establishment of culturally appropriate goals; selection of culturally appropriate interventions; facilitation of career decision making and clarification; and implementation.

The career development processes of African American women cannot be conceptualized in isolation from cultural influences. Fouad and Bingham (1995) illustrated the cultural embeddedness of career identity as a series of five concentric circles. From the center to the outermost circle, these influences consist of: a core (that is, genetic and biological factors that are immutable); gender (that is, role expectations); family (that is, culturally defined familial values); racial or ethnic group issues (that is, racial or ethnic identity development and worldview); and dominant/majority group issues (that is, societal barriers such as racism and sexism). Because these influences are not entirely independent, Bingham and Ward (2001) proposed that a nautilus or a spiral would more accurately illustrate the confluence of various cultural factors on the career identity development of African American college women.

Social cognitive career theory (Lent, Brown, and Hackett, 1994) has also been offered to account for the influence of personal, contextual, and social cognitive factors on the career development processes of diverse cultural groups. In fact, Gainor and Lent (1998) found that an array of background variables were associated with black undergraduates' career interests and career choice intentions. These researchers noted that the findings of their study could help counselors to expand their understanding of factors that might inhibit and promote black college students' full participation in college and in the workplace. When applying the findings to African American college women, it seems particularly important to consider the role of gender-role socialization experiences as a salient background variable that could influence various career development issues. For example, at the college or university level, some African American women may already be negotiating career development issues with regard to not having the option of not working, struggling in an academic major with few African American female professional role models, or being unintentionally dissuaded from career aspirations most commonly attained by white males (for example, becoming a chief executive officer of a large corporation).

Career counseling with African American college women entails assuming a broad contextual perspective. Thus, career-related interventions should be systemic as well as personal (Murry and Mosidi, 1993). Peer mentoring programs for African American college women may allow these women an opportunity to share and relate to peers from the same ethnic group. Outreach interventions, such as inviting prominent African American professionals to speak to and mentor African American women, especially those in math and science careers, may also foster these women's ability to attain their career aspirations. Because of cultural stigmas about formal mental health intervention, counselors might wish to address career issues in the context of a workshop or presentation with an existing group of African American female college students, such as a sorority, club, or religious group (Bingham and Ward, 2001). On a systemic level, counselors may want to encourage senior student affairs administrators to direct intensive recruitment and retention efforts toward African American female and male faculty, to create more diverse atmospheres on predominantly white college campuses and to identify and attend to potentially discriminatory academic and institutional practices through minority affairs offices.

Personal, Academic, and Career Issues of African American College Women: A Case Example

Brenda (a pseudonym) was a twenty-one-year-old, African American college sophomore majoring in elementary education at a large, predominantly white state university in the eastern United States. She presented at the counseling center on campus to address issues associated with her academic major and her sexual orientation. Brenda grew up in a small town near West Virginia. She described the town as conservative, with Orthodox Christianity as a core value of her hometown community. Brenda was the oldest of her parents' two children, and leaving home to attend a large university was a culture shock to her as well as to her parents and younger sister. She explained that her parents were very conservative and expected her to behave in ways that were consistent with their values. Thus, moving away from home and attending a university where Christian values may not be upheld was not what her parents expected or desired.

Prior to attending college, Brenda worked for two years as a receptionist for her father's auto body business. Her mother was not employed outside the home, but she engaged in volunteer activities with their church. While working for her father, Brenda decided that she wanted to pursue a degree in elementary education because she wished to teach children in an urban school setting. It was also during this time that Brenda began to recognize that her sexuality was not consistent with what her parents and others in her community had expected. Brenda reported that she was never interested in dating men, unlike some of her female friends from high school. Rather, she found herself sexually attracted to women exclusively. Brenda did not confide in anyone about her sexuality until she was ready to leave for college. When Brenda told her parents about her sexual attraction to women, they became outraged and demanded that Brenda attend church on a regular basis while at home and read the Bible daily in order to be "delivered from evil."

While at college, Brenda experienced some social difficulties adjusting to her new environment. Although she performed well academically, she did not socialize much with her peers because of the treatment she received from them because of her sexual orientation. The few interactions that she had had with African American students had been generally unpleasant because they had tried to set her up on a date with one of the guys on campus, despite her insistence that she was a lesbian. Moreover, there were times when Brenda believed that her white professors expected poor academic performance from her because she was black. There were also instances in which others would convey to her that she was too outspoken as a woman because she participated too frequently in her classes and in a small women's organization on campus. Because of these types of oppressive experiences, Brenda had become increasingly concerned about the ways in which her multiple oppressed identities (as an African American person, a woman, and a lesbian) would affect her career choice to be an elementary school teacher.

Counseling sessions with Brenda centered on discussing her feelings associated with being an African American lesbian. Brenda's feelings of depression, especially her social withdrawal, were associated with her difficulties in coping with others' reactions to her lesbian identity. Initial counseling sessions with Brenda revealed that she thought she would feel better about herself if she could somehow change how other people responded to her. She stated, "I wish people would get to know me as a person first without judging me as a lesbian. If they did, then my life would be so much easier." Brenda also expressed a great deal of frustration and pain associated with her family's and friends' reactions to her coming out, along with her feelings about not being connected to the African American community on campus because of her sexual orientation.

Brenda's counselor helped Brenda place her feelings within the larger context of American society. Specifically, Brenda and her counselor explicitly discussed issues such as racism, heterosexism, and sexism in her counseling sessions. Such discussions served to validate Brenda's feelings about being a member of multiple oppressed cultural groups and assisted her in understanding how issues of oppression had contributed to her current frustrations about being rejected by others for being an African American lesbian. Brenda's counselor also referred her to a lesbian women's support group on campus and a local predominantly black community church that was gay and lesbian affirmative, to assist her in obtaining support for her sexual identity. The insight that Brenda achieved through individual and group counseling was captured in a statement that she made in one of her individual counseling sessions: "There's not very much that's really wrong with me, but there's a lot that's wrong with a world that actively tries to oppress people's sense of who they are."

As Brenda began to develop more ego strength, she began to think about how she could realize and achieve her goal of becoming an elementary school teacher. With her counselor's assistance, Brenda joined some African American campus organizations and attended several conferences dealing with gay and lesbian issues in the workplace. Overall, the counselor assisted Brenda in understanding her feelings and concerns within the societal contexts in which she lived and helped to promote Brenda's ego strength regarding both her personal and professional functioning and development.

Summary

College personnel working with African American college women must be cognizant of the personal and systemic variables that may affect these women's experiences and how these experiences might be manifested. African American college women have been found to seek support from compartmentalized offices and resources on campus, such as financial aid offices, student health centers, academic advising and career counseling offices, and dormitory staff, in addition to mental health centers (June, Curry, and Gear, 1990; Schweitzer, Griffin, Ancis, and Thomas, 1999). Hence, college counseling centers, in particular, may benefit from greater collaboration with a broad array of related offices and services on campus.

College counselors might also assist African American college women through the use of systemic interventions that could include advocating for these students against various forms of institutional discrimination on campus (for example, biased class content and grading policies) (Constantine and Watt, 2002; Young and Rogers, 1991). These counselors might also need to take a more active role in providing nurturing and supportive environments for African American women on predominantly white college campuses through intensive minority recruitment strategies, promoting policies and norms that are reflective of these students' cultural values, and developing personal, academic, and career interventions that are rooted in culturally congruent notions of help seeking.

References

Ancis, J. R., Sedlacek, W. E., and Mohr, J. J. "Student Perceptions of Campus Cultural Climate by Race." *Journal of Counseling and Development,* 2000, *78,* 180–185.

Bingham, R. P., and Ward, C. M. "Career Counseling with African American Males and Females." In W. B. Walsh, R. P. Bingham, M. T. Brown, and C. M. Ward (eds.), *Career Counseling for African Americans.* Mahwah, N.J.: Erlbaum, 2001.

Boesch, R., and Cimbolic, P. "Black Students' Use of College and University Counseling Centers." *Journal of College Student Development,* 1994, *35,* 212–216.

Brown, S. P. "Images of Me: A Model to Promote Retention of Black Female Students on Predominantly White Campuses." *Journal of College Student Development,* 1994, *35,* 150–151.

Brown, S. P., Lipford-Sanders, J., and Shaw, M. "Kujichagulia: Uncovering the Secrets of the Heart: Group Work with African American Women on a Predominantly White Campus." *Journal for Specialists in Group Work,* 1995, *20,* 151–158.

Constantine, M. G. "Predictors of Satisfaction with Counseling: Racial and Ethnic Minority Clients' Attitudes Toward Counseling and Ratings of Their Counselors' General and Multicultural Counseling Competence." *Journal of Counseling Psychology,* 2002, *49,* 255–263.

Constantine, M. G., and Arorash, T. J. "Universal-Diverse Orientation and General Expectations About Counseling: Their Relation to College Students' Multicultural Counseling Expectations." *Journal of College Student Development,* 2001, *42,* 535–544.

Constantine, M. G., Chen, E. C., and Ceesay, P. "Intake Concerns of Racial and Ethnic Minority Students at a University Counseling Center: Implications for Developmental Programming and Outreach." *Journal of Multicultural Counseling and Development,* 1997, *25,* 210–218.

Constantine, M. G., Robinson, J. S., Wilton, L., and Caldwell, L. D. "Collective Self-Esteem and Perceived Social Support as Predictors of Cultural Congruity Among Black and Latino College Students." *Journal of College Student Development,* 2002, *43,* 307–316.

Constantine, M. G., and Watt, S. K. "Cultural Congruity, Womanist Identity Attitudes, and Life Satisfaction Among African American College Women Attending Historically Black and Predominantly White Institutions." *Journal of College Student Development,* 2002, *43,* 184–194.

Fouad, N., and Bingham, R. P. "Career Counseling with Racial and Ethnic Minorities." In W. B. Walsh and S. H. Osipow (eds.), *Handbook of Vocational Psychology.* Mahwah, N.J.: Erlbaum, 1995.

Gainor, K. A., and Lent, R. W. "Social Cognitive Expectations and Racial Identity Attitudes in Predicting the Math Choice Intentions of Black College Students." *Journal of Counseling Psychology,* 1998, *45,* 403–413.

Giles-Gee, H. F. "Increasing the Retention of Black Students: A Multimethod Approach." *Journal of College Student Development,* 1989, *30,* 196–200.

Gloria, A. M., Robinson Kurpius, S. E., Hamilton, K. D., and Willson, M. S. "African American Students' Persistence at a Predominantly White University: Influences of Social Support, University Comfort, and Self-Beliefs." *Journal of College Student Development,* 1999, *40,* 257–268.

Hendricks, F. M. "Career Counseling with African American College Students." *Journal of Career Development,* 1994, *21,* 117–126.

June, L. N., Curry, B. P., and Gear, C. L. "An Eleven-Year Analysis of Black Students' Experience of Problems and Use of Services: Implications for Counseling Professionals." *Journal of Counseling Psychology,* 1990, *37,* 178–184.

Kenney, G. E. "Multicultural Investigation of Counseling Expectations and Preferences." *Journal of College Student Psychotherapy,* 1994, *9,* 21–39.

Lent, R. W., Brown, S. D., and Hackett, G. "Toward a Unified Social Cognitive Theory of Career/Academic Interest, Choice, and Performance." *Journal of Vocational Behavior,* 1994, *45,* 79–122. Monograph.

Lucas, M. S. "Personal, Social, Academic, and Career Problems Expressed by Minority College Students." *Journal of Multicultural Counseling Development,* 1993, *21,* 2–13.

Mau, W-C., and Fernandes, A. "Characteristics and Satisfaction of Students Who Used Career Counseling Services." *Journal of College Student Development,* 2001, *42,* 581–588.

Murry, E., and Mosidi, R. "Career Development Counseling for African Americans: An Appraisal of the Obstacles and Intervention Strategies." *Journal of Negro Education,* 1993, *62,* 441–447.

National Center for Education Statistics, U.S. Department of Education. *Digest of Education Statistics.* Washington, D.C.: U.S. Government Printing Office, 1998.

Nickerson, K. J., Helms, J. E., and Terrell, F. "Cultural Mistrust, Opinions About Mental

Illness, and Black Students' Attitude Toward Seeking Psychological Help from White Counselors." *Journal of Counseling Psychology,* 1994, *41,* 378–385.

Schweitzer, A. M., Griffin, O. T., Ancis, J. R., and Thomas, C. R. "Social Adjustment Experiences of African American College Students." *Journal of Counseling and Development,* 1999, *77,* 189–197.

Stage, F. K., and Hamrick, F. A. "Diversity Issues: Fostering Campus Wide Development of Multiculturalism." *Journal of College Student Development,* 1994, *35,* 331–336.

Sue, D. W., Arredondo, P., and McDavis, R. J. "Multicultural Counseling Competencies and Standards: A Call to the Profession." *Journal of Multicultural Counseling and Development,* 1992, *20,* 64–88.

Terrell, F., and Terrell, S. "Race of Counselor, Client Sex, Cultural Mistrust Level, and Premature Termination from Counseling Among Black Clients." *Journal of Counseling Psychology,* 1984, *31,* 371–375.

Thomas, D. A., and Alderfer, C. P. "The Influence of Race on Career Dynamics: Theory and Research on Minority Career Experiences." In M. B. Arthur, D. T. Hall, and B. S. Lawrence (eds.), *Handbook of Career Theory.* Cambridge, England: Cambridge University Press, 1989.

Thompson, C. E., Worthington, R., and Atkinson, D. R. "Counselor Content Orientation, Counselor Race, and Black Women's Cultural Mistrust and Self-Disclosures." *Journal of Counseling Psychology,* 1994, *41,* 155–161.

Tomlinson, S. M., and Cope, N. R. "Characteristics of Black Students Seeking Help at a University Counseling Center." *Journal of College Student Development,* 1988, *28,* 65–69, 1994.

Trippi, J., and Cheatham, H. E. "Effects of Special Counseling Programs for Black Freshmen on a Predominantly White Campus." *Journal of College Student Development,* 1989, *30,* 35–40.

Trippi, J., and Cheatham, H. E. "Counseling Effects on African American College Student Graduation." *Journal of College Student Development,* 1991, *32,* 342–349.

Utsey, S. O., Adams, E. P., and Bolden, M. "Development and Initial Validation of the Africultural Coping Systems Inventory." *Journal of Black Psychology,* 2000, *26,* 194–215.

Watson, L. W., and Kuh, G. D. "The Influence of Dominant Race Environments on Student Involvement, Perceptions, and Educational Gains: A Look at Historically Black and Predominantly White Liberal Arts Institutions." *Journal of College Student Development,* 1996, *37,* 415–424.

Whaley, A. "Cultural Mistrust and Mental Health Services for African Americans: A Review and Meta-Analysis." *Counseling Psychologist,* 2001, *29,* 513–531.

Young, R., and Rogers, G. "The Impact of an Early Advising Program on the Success of Black Freshmen and White Freshmen." *Journal of College Student Development,* 1991, *32,* 375–376.

MADONNA G. CONSTANTINE *is professor in the Department of Counseling and Clinical Psychology at Teachers College, Columbia University.*

TAWANDA M. GREER *is staff psychologist at the Wright State University Counseling Center in Dayton, Ohio.*

An overview and context of holistic practices for serving African American women is presented. The needs, expectations, and aspirations of this population are addressed. Examples of and recommendations for programs and services are provided.

5

Programming Needs and Student Services for African American Women

Alexandria M. Rosales, Dawn R. Person

Increasing diversity of U.S. college students has stimulated renewed efforts to support these historically invisible and marginalized communities (Jackson, 1998). Recently, African American males have been the focal point of discussions of status, retention, and support (Malveaux, 2002; Turner, 2001). Although there is a need to focus on this at-risk group, continuing to ignore the needs of African American women, who represent the majority of the African American undergraduate population (Ntiri, 2001) and educational gains in the African American community (Sandham, 1997), is shortsighted. Black women are admitted, are retained, and graduate at a higher rate than previously reported, but their career choices often lead to less prestigious positions and less earning power (Cohen and Nee, 2000) than those attained by their white counterparts. Also, many African American women are lost from higher education as a result of structural, environmental, or sociocultural factors or combinations thereof that preclude educational and career achievements.

The myth that black women have achieved high levels of educational and career attainment over the past twenty years may contribute to the lack of attention by colleges and universities. Sokoloff (1992) presents a strong argument that dispels this myth. When black women are compared to white men, the lack of movement toward achievement and parity is obvious. Usually, black women are compared to white women and black men or other oppressed groups. These comparisons have led institutions to focus on women and black men, but the needs of black women have gone virtually unnoticed. Black women are either labeled and responded to as "blacks" or "women" (Schwartz and Bower, 1997) but rarely viewed and understood fully as "black women".

Institutional responsiveness to the needs of African American women is critical to their overall college achievement. Allen (1992, cited in Jackson, 1998) found that student perceptions of institutional support and responsiveness to their needs were linked to their college success. Previous student educational achievement had less impact; therefore, examining institutional responses to African American women in college is essential to providing necessary supports for academic success. These talented and eager female learners feel ignored and isolated by their institutions when there are insufficient services and programs (Moses, 1989) to assist them in reaching their full potential.

Discerning African American women students, their characteristics, experiences, self-perceptions, responses to perceived perceptions of others, and comfort level with their institution provides a foundation for programs and services. Institutions, regardless of their size, type, or mission, have a responsibility to respond to the ever-changing needs of black women students.

Diversity Within the Population of Black Women

Although African American women have a shared heritage, their experiences vary greatly; however, these differences often are ignored (Greene, 2000). Areas of diversity include age (for example, traditional- and nontraditional-age students), socioeconomic background and status, sexual orientation, visible and invisible disabilities, spirituality and religious belief systems, and family responsibilities. Like all other students, black women enter colleges and universities at different stages of their lives based on different motives, reasons, and goals. However, considering race, gender, and culture, the largest number of students of color at both undergraduate and graduate levels are black reentry females (Ntiri, 2001).

Although there have been advances in socioeconomic status for black women, the financial disparity between black women and their non–African American female counterparts persists. As a result, African American women are likely to view a college education as desirable for both personal and community economic improvement (Hamilton, 1996). Valadez (2000) studied rural African American women and found that their primary reasons for seeking an education were socioeconomic advancement and job preparation.

Other descriptive data on African American women identify issues and differences beyond age, gender, and class. Greene (2000) reported that research and literature on black lesbians is almost nonexistent. Available literature on this topic ties athletics and lesbian lifestyles to self-image (Person, Benson-Quaziena, and Rogers, 2001). Similar to the situation with black lesbians, there is a lack of emphasis on identifying and providing specific support services for black women with disabilities.

Since faith systems are embedded in the black community, African American women bring these traditions and practices with them to college as part of their survival systems (Knox, cited in Boyd-Franklin, 1989). African American women are involved in spiritual orientations ranging from Christianity and Catholicism to Buddhism and Islam. In Chapter Three, Sherry Watt provides an extensive overview of spirituality and faith development for African American women.

In addition, black women balance extensive responsibilities and multiple roles, including leadership within their family, extended family, and community (Boyd-Franklin, 1989; Hamilton, 1996). These roles may include one or more of the following: major caregiver, financial support of a household, spouse or life partner, single parent, or role model for younger siblings and community members. Balancing these roles and responsibilities adds to the pressures felt by black women in college (Ntiri, 2001).

The socialization process of African American women as nurturers of the community, in particular, is manifested in college. These women tend to value community, group cohesiveness and group socioeconomic mobility, and a commitment to uplifting others. They want to contribute to change on behalf of others as well as earn their degrees. Given this challenge, African American women need extensive support to succeed in college—support that is inclusive of their academic, social, cultural, economic, career, interpersonal, and intrapersonal needs. This broad-based support should provide a basis for these women to engage in a holistic educational experience in college.

Consistent with their diversity, African American women have a myriad of needs. The challenge in living with these needs is the struggle to maintain one's ethnic and gender identification while balancing other life responsibilities. Often addressed solely with respect to ethnicity or gender (Jackson, 1998), these life phenomena are too dynamic to be addressed from a singular perspective. Moving beyond this approach is possible if the needs, expectations, and aspirations of black female college students are identified and appropriate support is provided.

Response to College Experiences

Black female college students negotiate challenges beyond those of most college students, which often affect them emotionally, psychologically, and culturally. Initially, these women are likely to suffer anxiety over the lack of opportunities to enroll in an institution and obtain an education (Hamilton, 1996). The gap between the black community and many college and university communities contributes to a sense of isolation and alienation (Malveaux, 2002). In some cases, black women experience social disadvantages beyond race and gender. Cultural disadvantage also has been identified for black women in the South, a region of the country that has lagged behind the North and West (Schwartz and Bower, 1997).

Black women experience daily pressure from living in a less than inclusive and accepting society. This aspect is central to shaping their perceptions of and responses to external stimuli, including their families and communities. It operates when they take their initial steps toward college attendance, in selecting and applying to institutions, deciding on a major, campus involvement, and educational and career aspirations. Identity development (Chickering and Reisser, 1993; Cross, 1991; Helms, 1984; Phinney, 1990), intellectual and moral development (Gilligan, 1977; Kohlberg, 1972; Perry, 1970), transition into, through, and out of college (Astin, 1984; Fleming, 1984; Schlossberg, 1984; Watson and others, 2002), and establishment of meaningful relationships are all part of the process that leads to a healthy, well-rounded college experience (Fleming, 1984; Person and Christenson, 1996; Rendón, 1994). When African American women lack these elements in their college experience, their struggle becomes magnified, and environmental factors deter college success. A limited support system of peers and role models, monocultural curricular offerings, and institutional artifacts and traditions are examples of such environmental factors. Greene (2000) reported that these struggles stem from a majority culture that does not value women or people of color.

College Environmental Factors

Once enrolled in college, black women are often confronted with a general lack of sensitivity and understanding about their culture by faculty, staff, and other students. They also experience struggles associated with alienation due to stereotypical attitudes, unfamiliar values, ineffective teaching methods, and organizational approaches that may not support their efforts to succeed (Smith, 1989, p. 2). In a study by Jackson (1998), the theme of struggle was a constant when women recalled what it meant to be an African American woman in college. The students described experiences of "being oppressed; working harder than others to be successful; constantly having to prove oneself to others; not being able to complain; fighting negative stereotypes; and fighting battles against racism and discrimination" (p. 361).

Nettles (1986) found that perceived negative faculty attitudes toward students of color affected students' ability to become integrated into academic settings and to be successful. These perceptions can limit a student's sense of belonging and belief that they matter in the college environment.

A critical mass of black students is also important to the educational success of African American women. On some of our campuses, there are so few black women that little or no community exists and personal and identity development are without cultural and social contexts. This is a devastating position for many students to find themselves in when they enter college, one that most do not anticipate or have the coping mechanisms to manage.

Perceptions and Expectations

Institutions of higher education often impose different expectations on African American women from those they hold for African American men or white students of either sex. Faculty, staff, and other students often perceive black women as independent and aggressive. These women might feel pressured to take on this preconceived persona as a survival mechanism (Moses, 1989) and, in the process, lose a sense of genuineness in their self-concept.

Inter- and Intra-Personal Relationships

Central to this topic is the need for student affairs administrators and others working with students of color to recognize the impact of personal relationships within the African American campus community. Relationships take many different forms that include roommates, couples, social, buddies or friends, athletic teammates, fraternity and sorority members, and scholarly associates. The myriad of possible relationships can be challenging for African American women, but aside from the limited peers for social, academic, and athletic support, the most sensitive and critical relationship that may impact student retention and academic success is that of social connectivity that includes male-female relationships. This is particularly true when there is no critical mass of African American students, faculty, and staff at the institution. This issue of critical mass should be considered in terms of gender balance and representation within academic and social settings, such as the number of African Americans in a particular major, on a team sport, and even within a work setting.

African American students, especially on predominantly white campuses, struggle to develop healthy relationship patterns with each other. Interracial dating, the disproportionate ratio of men to women, and the intense focus on academics by African American women can serve as a deterrent to the development of healthy relationship patterns within the African American student community. The importance of male–female relationships for African American women envelops issues of self-concept (or self-worth) and academic motivation. African American women are less inclined to subordinate their studies to romance, compared to their white female counterparts; however, African American women do place great value on relationships with African American men (Holland and Eisenhart, 1990)

Another factor to consider when examining male-female relationships from the African American female perspective is the social dynamic of the campus. There is a tension on predominantly white campuses that often creates competition between African American females and other females for the attention and affection of African American males. These tensions often create resentment that can lead to fractures within the African American student community.

The difference in expectations concerning what constitutes a relationship is another variable that contributes to the tension between African American females and males. The inconsistencies in expectations and behaviors within the context of the relationship may lead to disappointment, hurt, and frustration.

Often other students and staff become involved in the intra-dynamics of individual relationships on campus, yielding a magnified state of confusion, aggravation, and drama for all involved. What was once a private relationship between two individuals becomes part of the public debate within the African American community. This situation leads to harm not only for the couple but for the community at large. When community members are apprised of the situation, they may become involved to some degree as a support network for the couple, or for one of the involved individuals. This phenomenon is particularly harmful when there is not a critical mass.

African American women and men may view the importance placed on sexual activity within the context of a relationship differently. This too can lead to misunderstandings, and African American women in particular to develop mistrust for their male counterpart. The choices African American women make within the context of a private relationship does not always remain within that setting. When information is shared or passed on regarding those choices, African American women feel betrayed by their partner. Again, this outcome leads to women doubting themselves and sometimes withdrawing from a community that offers support and a place of refuge. In fact, many African American women put their social needs and development on hold until after they graduate from college (Fleming, 1984).

When African American women date outside of their race, the community response is quite different from when African American men do the same. The intense scrutiny of other African American people contributes to emotional and mental strain for the women that choose this pathway. This is an added factor of stress and separation from the community.

Individuals who reduce the amount of time spent interacting with their identified network of support or student culture will often experience negative repercussions in the form of being ostracized or excluded from the group's culture. This is yet another example of the need for a critical mass of students so that opportunities exist to develop meaningful interpersonal and emotional relationships.

It has been noted that women and men have different communication styles. While this is not unique to African American relationships, the aforementioned dynamics combined with communication style differences add a dimension of complexity that is less prevalent in other relational phenomenons.

Effective ways to address relationship issues involve open and candid dialogue with expert facilitation. For example, useful methods include relationship workshops or programs, community-building retreats, and identity-nurturing support groups that are intentional in bringing male and female students together in a respectful and responsive manner. Workshops and programs on this topic almost always bring the community closer together. These programs can serve as vehicles for sharing, healing, and gaining new insights and perspectives on how to navigate within the social system of the institution and how to construct healthy relationships within the African American community.

Health Issues

Health issues are a major concern within the African American student population. Topics related to health include general and chronic illnesses, pregnancy, sexually transmitted diseases, eating disorders, and tobacco, alcohol, and drug use. African Americans exceed white Americans in mortality rates related to strokes, heart disease, cancer, diabetes, and murder (Hayes and Boone, 2001). African American women are affected by lupus, breast cancer, and HIV/AIDS more than other ethnic or racial female populations (Hayes and Boone, 2001). Given the prominent impact of these illnesses and conditions on the African American community in general and women in particular, research and health services targeting black women are necessary.

Pregnancy and sexually transmitted diseases (STDs) are factors that should be considered when discussing the persistence of black female college students. Generally, college students have been identified as a high-risk population for contracting sexually transmitted diseases resulting from capricious behaviors, particularly promiscuity and irregular condom use. Women and African Americans are considered to be particularly at risk for contracting STDs. One study focusing on black female college students reported an inconsistent use of condoms resulting in an increased probability of acquiring a STD. Pregnancy may also impede college progress and success (Lewis, Melton, Succop, and Rosenthal, 2000), contributing to stress and additional struggle.

Body image and eating disorders are also identified as major health issues among college students. Research shows that women suffer greater body image dissatisfaction than men, regardless of race or ethnicity (Demarest and Allen, 2000). White women suffer more frequently from negative body image and unhealthy eating behaviors than black women, but cases of African American women with eating disorders have increased (Abood and Mason, 1997; Nielsen, 2000).

Tobacco use, alcohol abuse, and drug use are constant issues on college campuses (Bower and Martin, 1999; Hestick, Perrino, Rhodes, and Sydnor, 2001). Tobacco use and drug use have declined, but alcohol consumption has been constant or increased (Bower and Martin, 1999). Hestick, Perrino, Rhodes, and Sydnor (2001) noted that cigarette use is lowest among African Americans when compared with other racial groups in college. This study found that most black college students say they only experiment with smoking. Another study on drug and alcohol consumption patterns of African American female athletes indicated that their drinking patterns were similar to those of college students in general, but their use of cigarettes was lower. The black female athletes in this study did not report use of drugs. This finding was noted as being similar to that for the general African American female student population (Bower and Martin, 1999).

Shifting Roles and Responsibilities

American women in college may be required to balance the responsibilities of being a wife, mother, and financial contributor (Ntiri, 2001) with those of being a student. In the case of many first-generation students, a lack of understanding can interfere with support for educational tasks. Sometimes families do not understand the time it takes to complete the educational process. As a result, family members might emphasize the need to secure a job or trade to contribute to the financial stability of the home. Such pressures might increase if the woman wants to pursue a graduate or professional degree (Schwartz and Bower, 1997). Pressure to work while attending college is a common condition that adds stress and consumes time that could otherwise be directed toward academics. It is also true, however, that the family can play an integral role in a student's success. In some instances, the family and community can provide the inspiration and support necessary to get through the challenges associated with college (Schwartz and Bower, 1997).

Aspirations

Fleming (1984) and Holland and Eisenhart (1990) studied African American women within larger studies of blacks and women, respectively. Both found that black women focused more on creating an economic base of support for themselves than on finding a life partner or mate. This finding supports many other studies that have examined socialization processes for African American women.

Black women are more likely than black men to be socialized to remain part of the community rather than focus on individual success (Weis, 1985). In addition, black women tend to aspire to professions that are less prestigious than those of their male peers (Grevious, 1985). Grevious concluded that constraints related to sex roles negatively affect career goals. Arnold (1993) found that structural forces such as race, class, and gender had a significant influence on underachievement for women enrolled in an urban public university. At the end of their collegiate experience, black women might have difficulty choosing a career. This indecisiveness has been attributed to apprehension about racism, sexism, or both (McCowan and Alston, 1998).

African American women also experience the weight of staying true to their culture and community (Jackson, 1998). They might believe that their individual education and achievement will result in an uplifting of the black community (Hamilton, 1996). They are likely to confront the challenge of maintaining a sense of self while being acculturated into a profession or field of study. Finding a place of self-affirmation as well as cultural affirmation is an ongoing dimension of balance and self-development for black women.

Programs and Services to Address Needs

Most of the programs and services to support and assist African American women are housed in one of six units: women's centers, multicultural centers, counseling and health services, cultural programs, student activities, and educational equity–academic support programs. This section of the chapter provides examples of programs offered for and about African American women that have proven over time to be successful. The programs highlighted in this section are examples known to the authors that have been effective support mechanisms for African American women. Many programs demonstrate collaborative efforts for serving women and were identified as part of a Web site search.

Women's centers usually offer programs and services for women such as resources on health issues, violence against women, changing roles of women in society, support groups, and encouraging academic success. Programs specifically for women of color are prominently displayed on Web pages and in program brochures and calendars of events. The Women's Resource Center at Michigan State University provides information on campus resources and events, as well as links to other sources of support, These links offer students access to information on financial aid and scholarships, grants and fellowships, health care, recreation, and entertainment.

The Women's Center at California State University–Long Beach features two programs. It provides a drop-in support group for African American women, facilitated by a counseling center psychologist. The Women's Center also offers a weekly workshop on black male-female relationships. Syracuse University has a support group for women of color that sponsors workshops related to professional and social concerns for women, coordinated by the Awakenings Women's Council.

Another source of support for African American women comes through the counseling centers on predominantly white campuses. The centers often offer counseling groups for black women, to assist them in coping with feelings of alienation and isolation. It is believed that this form of support contributes to student persistence and graduation (Mitchell, 2000). One example of a counseling group, the Sister-Friends group at the University of North Carolina, Greensboro, had about nine members in the late '90s and examined issues such as self-concepts, body image, spirituality, and educational and career plans. Members also explored their relationships with each other and coping mechanisms for campus life.

Mitchell (2000) reported that evaluation of this group program illuminated five recommendations for a successful program. Group facilitators needed to have knowledge of black women, bring together a diverse group of women, create a safe and confidential environment, address difficult issues, and encourage the women to focus on themselves.

Many examples of group counseling programs for African American women can be found at both public and private, large and small colleges and universities. For example, Lafayette College in Pennsylvania has a black women's support group that was developed in the late 1980s and is jointly coordinated by the college's counseling center and academic services. Both California State University, Long Beach, and California State University, Fullerton, have support groups for African American women that are jointly coordinated by the counseling center and the women's center.

The precursors to these counseling groups were African American support groups that promoted self-dedication, uplifting each other and the black race at large in the early 1900s (Johnson, 1999). Students, community members, and churchwomen organized these formal and informal support groups for African American women, including Alpha Kappa Alpha Sorority Incorporated, Delta Sigma Theta Sorority Incorporated, Links Incorporated, the 12th Street Bible Club, Daisy Belles, and Penny-Savers Clubs. Many of these groups are still active today. These efforts are multidimensional and focus on a broad range of issues such as education, community service, career development, spirituality, and cultural activities.

Mentoring programs involve African American faculty, alumni, and professionals as a source of support for students. Mentoring programs are viewed as an effective means of empowerment and as a way to support student persistence and retention (Munford, 1996; Person, 1996).

Another approach to serving African American women that has brought positive results for students and campuses is the creation of joint programs among institutions with limited African American student enrollments. Bryn Mawr, Swarthmore, and Haverford Colleges host a month-long joint orientation program for students of color (Roach, 1999). For the past seventeen years, Lehigh Valley colleges and universities have hosted a holiday formal for students of color. These events allow African American women to expand their social contacts and build a network of peers beyond their campus.

Although many educational and academic support programs offered by colleges and universities were not designed for African American women only, they provide needed services in academic, personal, career, and financial advising and counseling. Award programs and other recognition activities help to encourage African American women and spotlight their achievements and accomplishments. These programs offer role models, mentoring, and informal interactions that underscore community.

Offices for disabled student services and the informal and formal services for gay, lesbian, bisexual, and transgender students also can provide educational, social, and community support. Although these offices might have less experience providing services for African American women, they also provide an opportunity for new avenues of service delivery and support.

Conclusion

Recognition of the diversity of experiences and needs of African American women in college should lead to student and academic affairs seizing an opportunity to enhance the college community, black community, and future generations of African American college students. Through collaboration, the potential of both communities can be realized.

Many needs are yet to be addressed, however, and it is the responsibility of educational leaders to step up to the challenge by supporting each African American woman who enrolls in college. For many black women who make the decision to attend college, there are fear, conflict, challenge, and, often, limited support. We must offer more support for these achievers, create stronger support networks, and establish new programs of service to meet the diverse needs of African American women. No one service, one approach, or one program can meet all their needs.

References

Abood, D. A., and Mason, M. A. "Exploring Racial Differences in Body Dissatisfaction and Eating Attitudes and Behaviors." *American Journal of Health Studies,* 1997, *13*(3), 119–127.

Arnold, F. W. "Time Is Not on Our Side: Cultural vs. Structural Explanations of Black American Women Students' Achievement in the Urban, Nonelite University." *Urban Review,* 1993, *25*(3), 199–220.

Astin, A. W. "Student Involvement: A Developmental Theory for Higher Education." *Journal of College Student Personnel,* 1984, *25,* 297–308.

Bower, B. L., and Martin, M. "African American Female Basketball Players: An Examination of Alcohol and Drug Behaviors." *Journal of American College Health,* 1999, *48*(3), 129–133.

Boyd-Franklin, N. *Black Families in Therapy: A Multisystems Approach.* New York: Guilford Press, 1989.

Chickering, A. W., and Reisser, L. *Education and Identity* (2nd ed.). San Francisco: Jossey-Bass, 1993.

Cohen, C. J., and Nee, C. E. "Educational Attainment and Sex Differentials in African American Communities." *American Behavioral Scientist,* 2000, *43*(7), 1159–1207.

Cross, W. E. *Shades of Black: Diversity in African-American Identity.* Philadelphia: Temple University Press, 1991.

Demarest, J., and Allen, R. "Body Image: Gender, Ethnic, and Age Differences." *Journal of Social Psychology,* 2000, *140*(4), 465–472.

Fleming, J. *Blacks in College: A Comparative Study of Students' Success in Black and White Institutions.* San Francisco: Jossey-Bass, 1984.

Gilligan, C. "In a Different Voice: Women's Conceptions of Self and Morality." *Harvard Educational Review,* 1977, *47,* 481–517.

Greene, B. "African American Lesbian and Bisexual Women." *Journal of Social Issues,* 2000, *56(2),* 239–250.

Grevious, C. "A Comparison of Occupational Aspirations of Urban Black College Students." *Journal of Negro Education,* 1985, *54,* 35–42.

Hamilton, C. W. "Nature of Motivation for Educational Achievement Among African American Female College Students." *Urban Education,* 1996, *31*(1), 72–90.

Hayes, B. D., and Boone, L. R. "Women's Health Research at Historically Black Colleges and Universities." *American Journal of Health Studies,* 2001, *17*(2), 59–64.

Helms, J. E. "Toward a Theoretical Explanation of the Effects of Race on Counseling: A Black and White Model." *The Counseling Psychologist,* 1984, *12*(4), 153–164.

Hestick, H., Perrino, S. C., Rhodes, W. A., and Sydnor, K. D. "Trial and Lifetime Smoking Risks Among African American College Students." *Journal of American College Health,* 2001, *49*(5), 213–219.

Holland, D. C., and Eisenhart, M. A. *Educated in Romance: Women, Achievement, and College Culture.* Chicago: University of Chicago Press, 1990.

Jackson, L. R. "The Influence of Both Race and Gender on the Experiences of African American College Women." *Review of Higher Education,* 1998, *21*(4), 359–375.

Johnson, P. "Sister Circles." *Essence,* 1999, *30*(1), 126–131.

Kohlberg, L. "A Cognitive-Developmental Approach to Moral Education." *Humanist,* 1972, *6,* 13–16.

Lewis, L. M., Melton, R. S., Succop, P. A., and Rosenthal, S. L. "Factors Influencing Condom Use and STD Acquisition Among African American College Women." *Journal of American College Health,* 2000, *49*(1), 19–23.

Malveaux, J. "The Campus Gender Gap—A Women's Issue." *Black Issues in Higher Education,* 2002, *19*(1), 38.

McCowan, C. J., and Alston, R. J. "Racial Identity, African Self-Consciousness, and Career Decision Making in African American College Women." *Journal of Multicultural Counseling and Development,* 1998, *26*(1), 28–39.

Mitchell, N. A. "Sister-Friends: A Counseling Group for Black Female Undergraduates." *Journal of College Counseling,* 2000, *3*(1), 73–77.

Moses, Y. T. "Black Women in Academe: Issues and Strategies." Washington, D.C.: Project on the Status and Education of Women, Association of American Colleges, 1989.

Munford, R. L. "The Role of Mentoring in the College Experiences of Mature African American Women: A Qualitative Investigation." Paper presented at the annual conference of the American Psychological Association, Toronto, Canada, Aug. 1996.

Nettles, M., Thoeny, A., and Gosman, E. "Comparative and Predictive Analysis of Black and White Students' College Achievement and Experience." *Journal of Higher Education,* 1986, *57,* 289–318.

Nielsen, L. "Black Undergraduate and White Undergraduate Eating Disorders and Related Attitudes." *College Student Journal,* 2000, *43*(3), 353–370.

Ntiri, D. W. "Access to Higher Education for Nontraditional Students and Minorities in a Technology-Focused Society." *Urban Education,* 2001, *36*(1), 129–141.

Perry, W. *Forms of Intellectual and Ethical Development in the College Years: A Scheme.* New York: Holt, Rinehart, and Winston, 1970.

Person, D. R. "Recruitment and Retention of Black and Hispanic Math, Science, Engineering, and Technology Majors." Cross Case Analysis Final Report for the William Penn Foundation. New York: Teachers College, Columbia University, 1996.

Person, D. R., Benson-Quaziena, M., and Rogers, A. M. "Female Student Athletes and Student Athletes of Color." In M. F. Howard-Hamilton and S. K. Watt (eds.), *Student Services for Athletes.* New Directions for Student Services, no. 93. San Francisco: Jossey-Bass, 2001.

Person, D. R., and Christenson, M. "Understanding Black Student Cultures and Black Student Retention." *NASPA Journal,* 1996, *34*(1), 47–56.

Phinney, J. S. "Ethnic Identity in Adolescents and Adults: Review of the Research." *Psychological Bulletin,* 1990, *108*(3), 499–514.

Rendón, L. I. "Validating culturally diverse students: Toward a new model of learning and student development." *Innovative Higher Education,* 1994, *19,* 33–51.

Roach, R. "Succeeding on White Campuses." *Black Issues in Higher Education,* 1999, *15*(26), 42–48.

Sandham, J. L. "Big Boost in College Degrees to Blacks Reported." *Education Week,* 1997, *16*(23), 16.

Schlossberg, N. K. *Counseling Adults in Transition.* New York: Springer, 1984.

Schwartz, R. A., and Bower, B. L. "'Ain't I a Woman, Too?' Tracing the Experiences of African American Women in Graduate Programs in Education." Paper presented at the annual meeting of the American Educational Research Association, Chicago, March 24–28, 1997.

Smith, D. G. *The Challenge of Diversity: Involvement or Alienation in the Academy?* ASHE-ERIC Higher Education Report, *18*(5). Washington, D.C.: George Washington University, 1989. (ED 317 145)

Sokoloff, N. J. *Black Women and White Women in the Professions.* New York: Routledge, 1992.

Turner, M. R. "Don't Forget the Women." *Black Issues in Higher Education,* 2001, *10*(6), 34.

Valadez, J. R. "Searching for a Path out of Poverty: Exploring the Achievement Ideology of a Rural Community College." *Adult Education Quarterly,* 2000, *50*(3), 212–231.

Watson, L., and others. *How Minority Students Experience College.* Sterling, Va.: Stylus, 2002.

Weis, L. "Without Dependence on Welfare for Life: Black Women in the Community." *Urban Review,* 1985, *17,* 233–255.

ALEXANDRIA M. ROSALES is lead researcher for Honors in Biological Sciences, Howard Hughes Medical Institute program, at California State University–Long Beach and counselor for Student Support Services at California State University–Fullerton.

DAWN R. PERSON is professor and coordinator of the Student Development in Higher Education Program at California State University–Long Beach; program coordinator and codirector of the California State University/University of California–Irvine joint doctoral program in educational leadership; and a program evaluator and consultant.

6

The value of mentoring relationships among African American women in postbaccalaureate degree programs is emphasized and coupled with a discussion of the current shortage of same-race, same-sex mentors for African American female graduate and professional students.

Mentoring Relationships Among African American Women in Graduate and Professional Schools

Lori D. Patton, Shaun R. Harper

Mentoring has been considered one of the salient factors in academic and career success. On college and university campuses, it is common to find students who consider the mentoring relationships fostered with professors and advisers to be highly influential. Mentoring is particularly important on the graduate level, because emerging scholars and practitioners who intend to excel in their respective professions have the opportunity to make connections and learn how to successfully maneuver within their areas of specialization.

African American women in graduate and professional schools often find it difficult to locate suitable mentors with whom to build such connections. This chapter examines traditional definitions of mentoring through a review existing literature, provides a framework for understanding the mentoring needs of African American women, and highlights a research study that explored mentoring relationships among African American women in graduate and professional programs. Implications for strengthening mentoring relationships and better supporting the needs of African American women conclude the chapter.

Mentoring Defined

The term *mentor* was derived from Homer's epic tale *The Odyssey*. Odysseus selected his elderly friend, Mentor, to watch over his son Telemachus while he was away fighting in the Trojan War. Mentor was responsible for guiding, teaching, and offering counsel to young Telemachus in his father's absence. Although this is considered the origin of the term *mentor,* the word has taken on varied meanings in different fields over time. Mentors, according to Hill and Ragland (1995), "guide, train, and support a less skilled or experienced person called a novice, mentee, or protégé" (p. 72). Mentoring is a cornerstone in the success of graduate education and depends highly on student-faculty relationships propelled by trust, integrity, opportunity, and understanding.

Mentoring: The Missing Link for African American Women

As is mentioned throughout this volume, research on African American women in higher education is scarce. Consequently, few studies have been conducted that focus specifically on African American women and mentoring. Mumford's study (1996) found that African American women have a wide range of mentors that include friends, relatives, work-based supervisors, and professional colleagues who provide spiritual, emotional, financial, and educational advisement. The women deemed those mentoring relationships important to their personal and educational growth and career development. Blackwell's groundbreaking exploration (1983) of mentoring relationships among African American graduate and professional students found that women were less likely than men to have mentors. Similarly, more than three-fourths of the graduate students surveyed in Scandura and Williams' study (2001) reported having mentors, yet the female respondents were significantly less successful than the men in their quest to initiate, cultivate, and sustain meaningful mentoring relationships with faculty.

Jackson, Kite, and Branscombe (1996) found that African American women overwhelmingly preferred African American female mentors. However, they had a difficult time locating such women on predominantly white college and university campuses. Participating in a mentoring relationship with someone who looks like them, who has similar personal, professional, and scholarly interests and is devoted to their holistic experience and personal success as a graduate student in their chosen field, is keenly important for African American women and other students of color.

Mentoring relationships are vital to the facilitation of successful experiences for African American women and necessary in order for them to break the glass ceiling (Guido-DiBrito and Batchelor, 1988; Locke, 1997). However, because of the low numbers of African American female faculty and staff on campus, graduate women do not always have the opportunity to interact with other same-race women. According to Hughes (1988), "Minority women students have the most limited access to ethnic role models and mentors like themselves" (p. 65). Thus, African American female graduate and professional students who seek mentoring relationships are at an obvious disadvantage.

Locke (1997) suggests that a growing system of mentoring needs to be in place to alleviate the problem of too few African American female mentors on college and university campuses. Mentors could play a major role in the recruitment and socialization of younger scholars who are equipped with the skills requisite for success. In their study of African American women and mentoring, Howard-Vital and Morgan (1993) found that the majority of their respondents someday intended to become mentors. This finding is consistent with literature indicating that those who are mentored are more likely to serve as mentors in the future (Jacobi, 1991).

Alternative Support Sources

Given the scarcity of mentoring relationships among African American women in higher education, many graduate women go beyond their disciplines to seek out mentors for academic, emotional, and spiritual support (Essien, 1997). Informal networks may range from parents and family to church members, neighbors, and civic and professional organizations.

The establishment of support networks through family, friends, and the community is necessary to help women survive and excel in graduate programs. When they desire to have their issues placed at the forefront, African American women create or join networks with others who can relate to and understand their struggles, both personally and professionally. African American mothers have traditionally played significant roles in the mentoring of their daughters. During the college and graduate school years, many African American women rely on their mothers (who often live many miles away) to provide the inspiration, emotional support, and career advisement that is absent in mentoring relationships on campus. Other female family members, such as aunts, grandmothers, and cousins, also provide counsel and spiritual support to African American women during their pursuit of graduate and professional degrees.

African American women have also chosen to involve and align themselves with cohorts of other women who provide advice and a sense of sisterly connectedness. Since few networks exist on most campuses, many African American women derive their support from churches and informal community-based social groups. Many join what Reid-Wolfman (1997) refers to as "black secular organizations ranging from informal social clubs to structured national affiliates" (p. 165).

While formal networks could be made through campus organizations that have minority or gender-specific foci (for example, Black Law Student Association, Graduate Women in Business), many African American graduate women seek and build mentoring relationships with women external to their campuses. Wilkerson (1984) noted that professional associations have long been important networking outlets for women of color, because they provide an arena in which their voices can be heard and their issues can take priority. Professional associations and symposia afford African

American women the opportunity to interact with other positive and professional women of color, many of whom are highly regarded in their respective disciplines (Essien, 1997; Gregory, 1995; Miller and Vaughn, 1997). These women sometimes hold major leadership positions in other professional associations, including presidencies. Because the number of African American women in major leadership positions on college and university campuses is dismal at best, seeing other women of color in high-profile positions in professional associations motivates graduate women and confirms for them that success and respect in their chosen professions are attainable. Moreover, female-focused association committees (for example, the ACPA Standing Committee for Women, the AERA Research on Women and Education Special Interest Group) are valuable avenues for African American women who wish to learn from and foster long-lasting mentoring relationships with positive female role models.

In a study of African American female college presidents and chief executive officers, Sanford-Harris (1990) found that participants were actively involved in a variety of professional, civic, and social organizations, including the four national historically black sororities. Giddings (1988) suggests that these organizations have always been important sources of leadership training for black women, whose opportunities to acquire such skills through other organized campus and community groups are few (p. 16). Women who join these organizations during their collegiate or postundergraduate years are exposed to opportunities for involvement and a host of leadership experiences.

In addition to providing outlets for leadership development, black sororities also affect the career development of their members. One of the greatest benefits of membership is the lifelong network that is established among members, both locally and globally. These networks enhance graduate school options, career advancement, and job mobility. According to Berkowitz and Padavic (1999), "the idea of seeking strong, professional Black women as role models and possible mentors was a recurrent theme for these college [sorority] women, who spoke of ties with graduate chapters as a way to gain access to successful African Americans" (p. 10). The African American women in their sample also noted that sorority affiliation was part of their identity and would forever serve as a source of support and networking, even beyond the undergraduate years.

Reflections on Mentoring Relationships

This section is devoted to discussing the findings of a research study conducted to learn about contemporary mentoring experiences among African American women in graduate and professional schools. Individual, semistructured interviews were conducted with African American female students in postbaccalaureate degree programs in law, education, business, and the humanities at a large, predominantly white research university.

Half of the women were not engaged in mentoring relationships with other African American women, while the other half identified same-race women who served as mentors. Those without African American female mentors were asked about their mentoring relationships in general, while the others were asked questions pertaining specifically to the mentoring relationships they had with African American women. After reflecting on their personal experiences, the participants shared their thoughts on the value of having an African American female mentor, as well as the importance of same-sex mentoring among African American women.

The results of the study highlighted some important aspects of African American graduate women's perceptions of their mentoring relationships. While each had different mentoring experiences, several similarities existed among the women regardless of whether they had an African American female mentor.

The Value of African American Female Mentors. Overwhelmingly, the women in the study felt that having an African American female mentor would be a rich and unique experience. Although half of the participants did not have same-race female mentors, they were able to pinpoint the characteristics that would set an African American female mentor apart from others. The women stated that only an African American woman could understand the complex intersection of race and gender in the academy and society. They felt they could establish a deeper, more meaningful connection with her because of her firsthand life and academic experiences. Also, she could provide advice to help them avoid professional pitfalls while being a sister and a friend. Reportedly, these characteristics were rare or unavailable in mentoring relationships with men and mentors from other racial or ethnic backgrounds.

An interesting characteristic that emerged among those engaged in mentoring relationships with African American women was the concept of mothering. Those participants felt their mentoring relationship resembled that of a mother and daughter. They referred to their mentors as second mothers or described the women as comparable to their mothers. These maternal mentoring relationships consisted of nurturing, care, concern, worry, and honesty. In additional to emotional support, the mothering role in mentoring proved to be effective in helping the participants learn survival skills such as how to maintain professionalism, dress properly, successfully navigate political environments, and reject negative stereotypes that have been traditionally used to characterize African American women.

When available, the participants perceived African American female faculty to be extremely valuable; no mention was made of African American female staff or administrators. An African American faculty woman is in a perfect position to teach about the politics of the academy, both within and beyond the department, the participants noted. Furthermore, she can use her experiences and knowledge to shape positive self-concepts among female graduate and professional students while encouraging them to recognize their full potential as scholars and future career women in academe.

Explaining the Void. Many of the participants explained why so few African American women serve in mentoring roles. The most frequently cited reason was the absence of African American women in their academic departments. Many were pursuing postbaccalaureate degrees in programs that employed no African American female instructors. Thus, they had a limited pool from which to select same-race, same-sex mentors. Two additional concerns raised regarding the lack of African American female mentors, particularly faculty women, was the strong focus that these women placed on earning tenure and pleasing the white majority in their departments. These women were perceived as too busy and disproportionately loyal to research commitments. They placed their efforts more on personal and scholarly obligations and rarely reached out to graduate women. Participants also commented that negative reputations of faculty advanced by previous graduate students played a key role in their reasons for not approaching African American female faculty.

The participants' comments suggest that African American women in higher education must balance striving to achieve personal goals and ensure job security with attempting to help graduate women achieve their goals and offset the pressures of the academic environment. Ironically, some of the women who had access to potential African American female mentors did not make a concerted effort to build mentoring relationships. This was particularly true of the participants who were studying in fields not traditionally recognized for having large numbers of African American women (for example, business). Those who were not engaged in mentoring relationships with same-race women were sometimes unwilling or had not thought seriously about seeking an African American female mentor within another department (including nonacademic student services offices) because it was important to have a mentor who shared their academic interests.

Cultural Difference. Participants agreed that most traditional definitions of mentoring barely scratch the surface in the context of African American women. Providing academic guidance and career advice, while important, were not the only functions of a mentor, they believed. The participants acknowledged other components such as nurturing, mothering, and culturally relevant counsel—roles that could best be played by another African American woman. The participants also deemed trust to be an important function of mentoring. They expressed a desire to be able to share personal issues as well as academic and career concerns with their mentors in confidence. The women did not think a culturally different mentor would be as trustworthy. They felt that an African American woman would better relate to their experiences. She would understand their tears, their failures, and their triumphs, both in graduate school and outside academe. In particular, they did not believe a white mentor, male or female, could understand the depth of being an African American woman in general and in their respective areas of study specifically.

The responses regarding trust can be directly related to a "culture of dissemblance." Clark Hine (1995) describes this as "the behavior and attitudes of black women that creates the appearance of openness and disclosure, but actually shields the truth of their inner lives and selves from their oppressors" (p. 380). Many of the women, particularly those in mentoring relationships with white faculty and staff, felt like they had to portray an image of "being okay" or not having any "real problems." They were not willing to show their white mentors their personal side because it could reinforce negative perceptions of weakness or incapability of handling the rigors of graduate school. One participant noted, "I don't share too much with them other than what's going on with me academically and professionally, and that's the end of it. . . . That may not be a fair relationship, because I'm not letting them in all the way. I've cried on the phone with my black mentor, but I would never think of doing that in the presence of somebody else who's not like her. Often, crying is a sign of weakness—people have labeled it as such—and so I think they would misinterpret my tears."

The participants sought a sense of comfort in knowing that their personal business would remain confidential in their mentoring relationships. This assurance was often lacking in their relationships with culturally different mentors; therefore, they refrained from revealing certain parts of themselves and their struggles. Their responses further prove that African American women in the academy are unable to comfortably express themselves, their thoughts, and their true feelings for fear of being ridiculed, misunderstood, and misjudged.

Seeking Valuable Alternatives. The women in this study also mentioned other types of mentoring relationships they had experienced. They discussed the impact of peer mentoring as they pursued their graduate and professional degrees. Quite often, these peers were African American women from other graduate programs throughout the university. In many instances, the participants were the sole or one of few African American female graduate students in their academic department. Despite disciplinary differences, women across programs joined together to offer peer mentoring and support. "They can't necessarily advise me on what to do, but at least I know there is somebody who is in the struggle with me; that makes it a little bit better," one student noted. While a same-sex peer may not have been as knowledgeable about certain things, she could serve as a culturally familiar sounding board and someone to whom a woman could vent. The participants' remarks were consistent with Carroll's assertions: "Black women have few role models with whom to identify in developing healthy self-concepts. The great majority of their professors are White men, or, if they take Black studies courses, Black men. Rarely do they see Black women in responsible academic or administrative positions; and so students must look to each other for support and role models. As a result, they often form peer groups similar to extended structures" (1982, p. 119).

Peers were particularly important for women who did not have African American female mentors. Relationships with their peers served as a way of compensating for the mentoring they were not receiving from African American female faculty and staff. Their same-race female peers formed a sister circle that the women used for fellowship and to support one another.

Also, the women in this study viewed their family members—specifically their mothers and aunts—as mentors. They commented that whether their mothers had received a formal education or not, it was good to have familial support and someone who would just listen and understand. Furthermore, the lessons that their mothers taught extended beyond the academy and into their world experiences. "Even if they do not specifically understand the process, they always are willing to lend a word about how to interact and deal with people. . . . so it's always good to call home and still get those homegrown remedies on how to go through life and deal with things."

Committed to Giving Back. Each woman expressed the importance of serving as a mentor to other African American women, regardless of whether she had a relationship with an African American female mentor. They felt that a large responsibility in mentoring was serving as a role model and presenting a positive image to young African American women. The participants owed it to themselves and to the African American women who aided in their success to reach back and pull others along. A doctoral student in education offered these comments: "All my life, from undergraduate through two master's degrees and now a Ph.D., there was always one black woman who came into my life—whether she was a custodian, the vice president, a faculty member, or the lady who worked in the cafeteria—who gave me tips and guided me. So, I've always been compelled to do those same things for any black female student I come in contact with." Realizing the challenges they faced in finding and maintaining meaningful mentoring relationships with other African American women, the participants were earnest in their desire to give back to the black community by serving as mentors to other women, particularly African American female undergraduates.

Recommendations

Mentoring relationships among African American women are vitally important. While numbers of African American women in faculty and administrative roles are low, the role that these women can play in assisting future generations of women in the academy is essential. The participants who were engaged in mentoring relationships with African American women could not say enough about the impact of these women on their lives. Those who did not have African American female mentors noted the positive impact that such a presence could have on their success in graduate and professional school and in their future careers. Unarguably, a large responsibility must be shouldered by African American women to foster mentoring relationships with graduate and professional students. So what might be done to help create effective mentoring relationships for African American female graduate and professional students? Following are some approaches that can be taken by faculty, staff, and students.

Recommendations for African American Women Faculty and Staff. It may be necessary for African American women faculty, staff, and administrators to initiate outreach to same-race graduate women on campus. Reaching out requires time. Making room within a weekly schedule to meet one-on-one with students or to create a sister circle with two or three African American graduate women, particularly those who are in departments that have no African American female faculty or staff, could be immensely helpful. In addition, encouraging these women to create a peer-mentoring circle allows them to depend on each other for support and lessens the burden that on numerous occasions has weighed down African American female mentors. It is also important for African American female faculty and administrators to stress that whether they have experience in a particular profession or not, they can serve as a resource, friend, confidante, and sister to graduate women. This is particularly important for staff and administrators, because many participants in the study perceived nonacademic mentoring relationships as not valuable or unworthy of exploration. As schedules tighten and responsibilities pile on, African American female faculty and administrators must continue to reflect on their previous mentoring experiences and the factors that contributed to their success and use those thoughts as a guiding motivation to reach out to same-race women in graduate and professional programs.

Recommendations for Graduate and Professional Students. African American graduate women must be willing to reach out to African American female faculty and administrators, both within and beyond their department. While a professor in sociology or the vice president for student affairs may not fully understand the plight of a female graduate student in biology, they both may offer valuable support and insight on successfully navigating environments in which African American female representation is dismal. They also may have long-standing relationships with African American female biologists on other campuses with whom they can connect the graduate student. Sometimes it takes student initiative to cultivate these cross-disciplinary connections. The sociologist who is very committed to supporting African American female graduate students may not even know that she has a sister in the biology program that is in need of mentoring.

Using fellow African American female graduate students as a peer-mentoring network can also help to put the stresses of graduate school into perspective. Given that many African American women are in academic programs where black women are grossly underrepresented and are sometimes the lone black woman in their program, they may consider the graduate and professional student organizations as potential places to connect with their same-race, same-sex peers from other academic programs. Students can also participate in professional associations and attend annual conferences to network with other African American women in their profession. Additional networks such as the church can be a resource for building a spiritual foundation, receiving encouragement, and connecting with African American women from the community. Furthermore, the black sorority network can be used to meet new women and build potentially meaningful mentoring relationships. African American graduate and professional women may also benefit from expanding their mentoring circle to include other-race or male mentors. While trust tends to be a major issue in such relationships, taking the initiative to approach university staff for assistance and slowly building a connection may eventually develop full-fledged mentoring relationships, despite racial, cultural, and gender differences.

Recommendations for Non–African American Faculty and Staff. Myers (2002) suggests that mentors do not have to be of the same race or gender as their mentees; however, they must be aware of the politics of difference. Mentors would need to be aware of the circumstances that could emerge as a result of race and gender, as well as how those characteristics alone set African American graduate and professional women apart from other students on their campuses. Given the extreme shortage of African American faculty and staff at predominantly white institutions, it is important that culturally different faculty and staff—especially white professors and administrators, who remain the majority—willingly reach out to assist African American graduate women, whether in a mentoring capacity or simply providing general guidance and encouragement. Non–African American faculty and staff must also be reflective in recognizing and alleviating the biases and stereotypes that they may personally hold regarding African Americans and respond more empathetically to the issues and concerns of this population. Furthermore, considering that trust issues tend to be a significant barrier, it is important that culturally different faculty and staff members ensure confidentiality when mentoring African American women.

Recommendations for Student Services Units. Several university departments and student services units can be instrumental in helping African American female graduate and professional students to locate mentors. For example, women's centers can work collaboratively with other campus offices to offer programs that allow African American female faculty, staff, and graduate students to interact socially (for example, a black women's tea or an African American female authors book club). The women's center may also take the lead in producing a directory of African American female faculty, staff, and students to be distributed to African American women across degree programs, including undergraduate programs. Alumni affairs offices may partner with academic units and the black cultural center to explore ways of better connecting African American alumnae with current graduate and professional students in mentoring capacities.

Institutions should also offer financial resources that can be used to off-set the expenses associated with attending professional conferences and symposia, because they tend to be marketplaces at which graduate women interact in, learn from, and cultivate long-lasting mentoring relationships with other African American women. Another suggestion for strengthening a university's relationship with African American women involves actively seeking and recruiting more African American female faculty and staff members. The dismal representation of African American faculty and staff at predominantly white institutions yields an extremely limited pool of same-race mentors for African American female graduate students. Simply making a concerted effort to meet the mentoring needs of this population would, at a minimum, communicate an institutional concern for the success of black women at the university and beyond.

References

Berkowitz, A., and Padavic, I. "Getting a Man or Getting Ahead: A Comparison of White and Black Sororities." *Journal of Contemporary Ethnography*, 1999, 27(4), 530–557.

Blackwell, J. E. "Networking and Mentoring: A Study of Cross-Generational Experiences of Black Graduate and Professional Schools." Atlanta: Southern Education Foundation, 1983.

Carroll, C. M. "Three's a Crowd: The Dilemma of the Black Woman." In G. T. Hull, P. B. Scott, and B. Smith (eds.), *All the Women Are White, All the Blacks Are Men, but Some of Us Are Brave: Black Women's Studies* (pp. 115–128). New York: The Feminist Press, 1982.

Clark Hine, D. "Rape and the Inner Lives of Black Women in the Middle West: Preliminary Thoughts on the Culture of Dissemblance." In B. Guy-Sheftall (ed.), *Words of Fire: An Anthology of African-American Feminist Thought*. New York: New Press, 1995.

Essien, P. "Black Women in the Sciences: Challenges Along the Pipeline and in the Academy." In L. Benjamin (ed.), *Black Women in the Academy: Promises and Perils*. Gainesville: University of Florida Press, 1997.

Giddings, P. *In Search of Sisterhood: Delta Sigma Theta and the Challenge of the Black Sorority Movement*. New York: Morrow, 1988.

Gregory, S. T. *Black Women in the Academy*. Lanham, Md.: University Press of America, 1995.

Guido-DiBrito, F., and Batchelor, S. W. "Developing Leadership Potential for Minority Women." In M. D. Sagaria (ed.), *Empowering Women: Leadership Development Strategies on Campus*. San Francisco: Jossey-Bass, 1988.

Hill, M. S., and Ragland, J. C. *Women as Educational Leaders: Opening Windows, Pushing Ceilings*. Thousand Oaks, Calif.: Corwin Press, 1995.

Howard-Vital, M. R., and Morgan, R. *African American Women and Mentoring*. Edinboro, Pa.: University of Pennsylvania, 1993. (ERIC Research Report, ED 360 425)

Hughes, M. S. "Developing Leadership Potential in Minority Women." In M. D. Sagaria (ed.), *Empowering Women: Leadership Development Strategies on Campus*. San Francisco: Jossey-Bass, 1988.

Jackson, C. H., Kite, M. E., and Branscombe, N. R. "African-American Women's

Mentoring Experiences." Paper presented at the annual meeting of the American Psychological Association, Toronto, Ontario, Aug. 1996.

Jacobi, M. "Mentoring and Undergraduate Academic Success: A Literature Review." *Review of Educational Research,* 1991, *61*(4), 505–532.

Locke, M. E. "Striking the Delicate Balances: The Future of African American Women in the Academy." In L. Benjamin (ed.), *Black Women in the Academy: Promises and Perils.* Gainesville: University of Florida Press, 1997.

Miller, J. R., and Vaughn, G. G. "African American Women Executives: Themes That Bind." In L. Benjamin (ed.), *Black Women in the Academy: Promises and Perils.* Gainesville: University of Florida Press, 1997.

Mumford, R. "The Role of Mentoring in the College-Experiences of Mature African American Women: A Qualitative Investigation." Paper presented at the annual meeting of the American Psychological Association, Toronto, Ontario, Aug. 1996.

Myers, L. W. *A Broken Silence: Voices of African American Women in the Academy.* Westport, Conn.: Bergin and Garvey, 2002.

Reid-Wolfman, B. "Light as from a Beacon: African American Women Administrators in the Academy." In L. Benjamin (ed.), *Black Women in the Academy.* Gainesville: University of Florida Press, 1997.

Sanford-Harris, J. "A Profile of Black Women College Presidents and Chief Executive Officers." Unpublished doctoral dissertation, Boston College, 1990.

Scandura, T. A., and Williams, E. A. "An Investigation of the Mentoring Effects of Gender on the Relationships Between Mentorship Initiation and Protégé Perceptions of Mentoring Functions." *Journal of Vocational Behavior,* 2001, *59*(3), 342–363.

Wilkerson, M. B. "Lifting as We Climb: Networks for Minority Women." In A. Tinsley, C. Secor, and S. Kaplan (eds.), *Women in Higher Education.* San Francisco: Jossey-Bass, 1984.

LORI D. PATTON is a doctoral student in the higher education program and director of multicultural outreach in the Office of Admissions at Indiana University Bloomington.

SHAUN R. HARPER is assistant professor of clinical education and executive director of the Doctor of Education Program in the Rossier School of Education, University of Southern California, in Los Angeles.

7

This chapter explores factors of concern for, and overall experiences of, African American female faculty and administrators, including salary issues, affirmative action, racism, sexism, homophobia, campus climate, isolation, tenure and promotion processes, and salary.

The Experiences of African American Women Faculty and Administrators in Higher Education: Has Anything Changed?

Carol Logan Patitu, Kandace G. Hinton

A search of databases for information on African American women faculty and administrators in higher education revealed a dearth of research on the topic. This paucity of literature and research reflects the scarcity of African Americans in academic affairs, student affairs, and other administrative positions. According to the *Digest of Education Statistics* (National Center for Education Statistics, 2002), in Fall 1999 African American women held only 5 percent (7,887) of the 159,888 executive, administrative, and managerial staff positions in institutions of higher education. Also, African American women represent only 2.5 percent (14,562) of the 590,937 full-time instructional faculty in degree-granting institutions (National Center for Education Statistics, 2002).

The research that has been conducted focuses on issues that affect retention, promotion and tenure, and job performance of middle- to senior-level African American women administrators and faculty. These studies identified issues such as racism, sexism, homophobia, climate, isolation, salary issues, coping strategies, and institutional ethos, and the impact of these and other issues on the lives and work of African American women (Allen and others, 2002; Delgado-Romero, Howard-Hamilton, and Vandiver, 2003; Edmundson, 1969; Kolodny, 2002; Jackson, 2001; James

---

Note that all respondent names used in this chapter are pseudonyms.

and Farmer, 1993; Mintz and Rothblum, 1997; Myers, 2002; Rusher, 1996; Smith and Stewart, 1983; Winkler, 1982).

In addition, Sagaria (2002) asserts that during administrative searches, institutions may be using a range of "filters" that tend to eliminate African Americans and other people of color from the hiring pool. Although there have been pioneering efforts, "little progress has been made in achieving [and maintaining] administrative positions" (Noble, 1993, p. 101).

Predominantly white institutions have not been particularly successful in recruiting and retaining black faculty, men or women. Patitu and Tack (1998) state: "Yet, even with all of the special attention that has been paid to their employment and advancement, women and minority faculty have not made significant headway in the academy; they continue to be clustered in disciplines considered to be traditional or 'feminine,' in the lower academic ranks, and in part-time or temporary positions" (p. 8).

Given the increasing number of students of color in institutions of higher education and given increasing efforts to develop multicultural learning communities on campus, these issues must be addressed. Black female faculty and administrators on predominantly white campuses can significantly influence the lives of students. One way in which students are affected by the presence of black women is through mentoring. African American female students who need and seek mentoring relationships often discover that those relationships are difficult to develop because of cultural differences between black women and white faculty and administrators and the lack of potential mentors who have experiences similar to those of black students.

Furthermore, the experiences of African American women in administrative and faculty roles is important because enrollment and persistence toward degree completion of African American students is linked to the number of African American faculty and administrators present on predominantly white campuses (Fleming, 1984; Gardiner, Enomoto, and Grogan, 2000). When minority students see African American and other minority faculty on campus, they believe that they can also succeed and hold professional positions.

This chapter uses data from two recent studies (Hinton, 2001; Patitu, 2002, unpublished raw data from study done for this chapter) to explore experiences and concerns of African American women faculty and administrators. Issues to be addressed include salary, affirmative action, racism, sexism, homophobia and heterosexism, campus climates, feelings of isolation, and tenure and promotion processes. These issues have surfaced over the years for African American faculty and administrators, which in turn led us to ask, "What has changed for African American faculty and administrators in higher education?" The rest of this chapter attempts to answer that question. We divide the discussion into two sections: the first addresses the experiences of African American women in administrative roles; the second addresses the experiences of African American women faculty.

African American Female Administrators

When asked to describe their experiences as African American women in administrative roles in higher education, participants in the research we conducted cited racism, sexism, and homophobia as particular concerns.

Racism. One of the questions left unanswered in the literature on African American women who are administrators is which avenue of discrimination is more salient, race or gender? Hinton (2001) interviewed five middle- and senior-level African American women in administrative roles at five different institutions (one public Research Extensive, one private Research Extensive, one regional comprehensive, one urban commuter, and one public two-year) and found that for these women, race was more salient in their efforts to retain their positions and seek promotion. One respondent believed that being a woman was less threatening to others than being African American. She stated, "My race overshadowed being a woman. Being a woman was nothing. I would be surprised if you don't find that African American women, because of their race, wrestle with issues as administrators that White women do not confront, because we are not seen like they are" (p. 126). Another participant, however, believed that racism and sexism were equally problematic.

Sexism. Despite some commonalities between sexism and racism in stereotyping (for example, devaluation and exclusion), "sexist and racist interpersonal and institutional processes also take crucially different forms" (Smith and Stewart, 1983, p. 3). Furthermore, racism and sexism have similar and differing effects on their targets. For most African American women, racism and sexism are not always distinguishable. Often they exist in tandem. This section of the chapter describes the processes and effects of sexism on the women who participated in this study.

Sunni Day, a coordinator of multicultural services at a small public two-year college, Lemon State, recalled that a white administrator pointedly told her that although she might perceive her treatment as racist, it is highly possible that sex could play a stronger role. Institutional sexism is evident at Lemon State in the fact that there were no female vice presidents, deans, associate deans, or assistant deans; "they are all White males." Sunni, in addition, has been excluded from positions of power by being denied director status (her position as coordinator was titled director for her male predecessors), which forced her to become dependent on white men to discuss and decide what was best for her office.

> There was a period when the vice-president that I reported to would only speak to me through my assistant because he is a man, and he didn't want to talk to me. So if there was something major that happened, I was the last to know. He would meet with my assistant and tell him things until I went off! I went off several times and told him "I've had enough of it; I'm the director, this is what you pay me to do; this is the position you have given me and I

want to be respected as that." That's how I was treated, which was not due to racism because my assistant is also Black—that was sexism. [Hinton, 2001, p. 136]

Homophobia. According to Collins (1998), "Race, class, and gender are the systems of oppression that most heavily affect African American women" (p. 225). However, the lived experiences of African American women include other oppressions, such as homophobia and heterosexism. Two of the women in Hinton's (2001) study, Sunni and Nikki, have been consistently involved in same-sex relationships.

Sunni did not disclose her sexual orientation in the workplace, except she did come out to an African American male colleague and friend, who, in turn, "outed" her to others, including students. Her experiences with homophobia have been painful and oppressive. As a result of her colleague's betrayal, Sunni experienced verbal attacks from students. Also, many of her on-the-job struggles since being outed could be linked to her sexuality; the interlocking elements of race, gender, and sexual orientation define much of who she is (Collins, 1998).

I've had people tell me, "you don't even know if the reason you're being treated this way is because you're Black, you're female," and now a third one is because of the fact that I enjoy the company of the same sex—I don't know what it is. [Hinton, 2001, p. 143]

What Sunni does know is that being outed caused her to lose the respect of some students. At a graduation recognition ceremony, an African American male student publicly insulted Sunni by suggesting that she was a man because of the rumors about her sexual orientation. The humiliation Sunni faced at this event did not end that night. "Some students acted like they didn't want to be in the same room with me. What was I going to do, attack them? Was I a monster or something?"(Hinton, 2001, p.143). The humiliation she suffered illustrates the level of disrespect that lesbians might expect, especially when it is compounded by race and gender prejudices.

Effects and Processes of Racism, Sexism, and Homophobia. Marginalization, lack of support, survival and coping skills, and transition and growth are the subthemes that provide a context for the work and life experiences of the women involved in the study just described. These subthemes also demonstrate the effects and processes of racism, sexism, and homophobia.

Marginalization is defined as any issue, situation, or circumstance that has placed these women outside of the flow of power and influence within their institutions. Three of the women, at various times during their professional careers in higher education, were placed at the periphery of the decision-making process, access to resources, and participation in their organizations.

Sunni Day, for example, was consistently excluded from weekly meetings with the vice president of student affairs that other directors participated in, because her title was shifted to coordinator (rather than director) of multicultural services when she accepted the position. As long as Sunni was classified within the college's organizational structure as a coordinator, she and the people she served would be denied a voice and power. She stated:

> As a director, I would be allowed to get in the inner circle of student services, which I have been intentionally left out of. It would allow us a voice to be heard and respected. I have been told that the dean of students is supposed to represent us. I run that office. . . . We are a legitimate office and no one can represent our office better than we can. All of the other directors meet weekly and share what's going on in student services. They have the opportunity to work together, to be on the same team. Only when there is a problem that they can't resolve with regard to African American students, are we called in to respond. And each time our response is a home run. They will do everything they can to make sure we're the last called, and no matter the challenge, we've handled it efficiently. [Hinton, 2001, p. 150]

Support is vital to African American women who work in hostile environments at predominantly white institutions (PWIs). The administrators in this study provided many examples of their need for professional and personal support in the administrative roles they were asked to perform. Lack of support, in some cases, caused them to be ineffective in their positions. Lack of support, for these women, came in the form of sexual harassment from an immediate supervisor, budget constraints, denial of programming to increase diverse student enrollment, verbal abuse from African American men, and simply being ignored, isolated, and alienated.

Aisha, a vice provost for student development at a private Research II institution, said she possessed a "no fear" attitude. Because she experienced much of the racism and sexism characteristic of the others' experiences, she too has had to learn coping and survival techniques to preserve her sense of personhood and sense of purpose. In addition, her strong faith in God and her prayer life, like those of the other four women, stand out as her main coping mechanism. Laughter and poking fun at racist behavior are other ways that Aisha copes.

> One of my girlfriends would always say that she would shake this one White administrator's hand, and he would wipe his hand off. So we had this deal that we would always shake his hand and make him wipe his hand off. But we were able to poke fun at it; it's not funny, but it's survival skills. You can get all mad and uptight or you can say you are a fool, 'cause I'm going on. [Hinton, 2001, p. 179]

Although these women experienced barriers associated with racism, sexism, and homophobia, they have persisted for decades in positions that they believe are their destiny. They have survived and coped because of parents, spouses, family, friends, colleagues, and supportive supervisors. They also shared that laughing, crying, praying, retreating, physical illness, a sense of self, and moving on were intentional and unintentional survival and coping methods.

To cope and survive in these environments, some of them retreated, some worked harder and smarter, some relied on support networks and faith in God and used prayer and spiritual development, while others invoked laughter and recalled pearls of wisdom from other black African American women, grandmothers, and holy scripture.

Because these women value their work and the experiences that have come with it, they also believe that they have made contributions to their professions. Transition and growth emerged from their perceptions of their ability and maturity over time. Juanita, an associate professor and the community liaison director for a large urban commuter university, has spent more than thirty-three years in higher education. Born in the late 1940s, she framed much of her story in a historical context because of the time period in which she grew up, the years she was in college, and the decade in which she began her professional life—the post–civil rights years.

> The desegregation movement in Maryland, during the '60s when I was in high school, helped to shape my perceptions of race and America. I marched, sat-in, prayed-in and [even] saw so many Black people attack each other. This gave me strong signals about how complex race is in America. Funny, though, what I saw and learned during that time really didn't kick in until very recently. That is, for twenty years I felt that if you kick the door down, people are likely to be sweet and welcoming when you get inside. Love was the answer then just as it is now. But it's so much more exciting kicking the door down. [Hinton, 2001, p. 186]

The transition and growth realized by these women demonstrate the contributions they have made to the higher education profession. Furthermore, their personal maturity has served them well in how they have changed the way they communicate and fight battles. The greatest change, however, has occurred within the women themselves. Possessing a fighter's mentality, they do not see themselves as victims. They do not hesitate to speak out against any injustice they face but are tempered by their wisdom and maturity. Yet, what each woman revealed about her particular struggles suggests that there is a need for African American women administrators at PWIs to have a voice, not just a place, in higher education administration. Their visibility and presence will only increase as policies and practices come to include an understanding of cultural and gender differences.

African American Women Faculty

Following are the results of the study conducted by Patitu (2002) on the experiences of African American women faculty.

Levels of Satisfaction with Their Experiences. African American faculty have been part of a revolving door in higher education. Patitu (2002) interviewed five faculty members at three different ranks (assistant professor, associate professor, professor) at different institutions (three worked at doctoral-granting research institutions, one worked at a four-year college, and one worked at a community college) about their experiences in higher education. Four of the respondents expressed overall satisfaction, although one noted that all eyes were watching her when she first got her job and another questioned why some have to do more than others. The fifth participant was very dissatisfied. Armetha, a professor who has been in a faculty position for fifteen years, commented:

> I was the first Black professor in the Registered Nursing Department. At first I was observed very closely by the other faculty members to make sure that I could "fit in" and perform at a high level in the position. They quickly discovered that in most cases I did the job at a much higher level than they did because I was willing to put in more time to ensure that. At present, I am very satisfied with my job. A couple of years ago I was offered the job of assistant chair of the department but declined because my salary would remain the same—just more administrative responsibility. I love teaching and interacting with students of all ethnic backgrounds and I really do feel that I make a difference in the lives of many of my students. I love to see the expression on Black students' faces when they see that there is a Black faculty member that they can relate to. [Patitu, 2002, raw data]

Linda, an associate professor who has been in her faculty position for seven years, stated that she is satisfied with her experience. She said, "I have excellent colleagues and a good working environment" [Patitu, 2002, raw data].

Tamara, who has been in her position for only three and a half years and who is in the midst of the tenure and promotion process, felt that her experiences have, for the most part, been positive. She is frustrated primarily with her institution's lack of commitment to diversity. She stated:

> I am frustrated sometimes when I sit in faculty meetings or engage in discussions with my students and colleagues and find that they are not as progressive in their thinking about diversity issues. I worry that my institution is behind the curve on how to recruit, mentor, and retain faculty of color in higher education. Universities have a tendency to hide behind the cloak of affirmative action lawsuits, rather than work to create viable, creative alternatives to achieving a diverse university. [Patitu, 2002, raw data]

Renee, the newest faculty member of the five, who has been in her position for only one year, is clearly dissatisfied. She is dissatisfied not only with
the location of her job but also with the community, which "seems to be
complacent about critical political and social issues that affect people of
color and the nation" (Patitu, 2002, raw data). Thus, she, too, is concerned
about commitment to diversity. She has decided to look for another position, to get away from her present institution. This is very unfortunate,
because Renee is the only African American faculty member in her program;
if she leaves, there will be no African American presence.

Tenure Status and Experiences. In tenure-track faculty positions, a
person must go through the tenure process to obtain permanent status.
Three of the respondents (Armetha, Rita, and Linda) had tenure; two
(Tamara and Renee) did not. When asked about their experiences in achieving tenure or working toward that goal, the respondents' perceptions varied. For some, there was no problem; for others, concerns included
conflicting information, unwritten rules, higher expectations for faculty of
color than others, and the absence of mentoring and direction from others.
They described more negative experiences than positive.

Armetha stated she had had no problems. She attributed this to her
context, a community college, where tenure and promotion might be less
complicated processes than at research universities.

> At the Community College level getting tenured is based primarily on
> involvement in college and professional activities and community service. In
> addition, I have received a Ph.D. and a Post-Masters Degree, which helped.
> Each time that I was up for promotion, I received it without any problems.
> [Patitu, 2002, raw data]

The other respondents, who served doctoral-granting or research universities, expressed frustrations and did not view the tenure and promotion
processes as problem-free. Linda, an associate professor, stated that the process was stressful and nitpicky, characterized by conflicting information.
She stated:

> Requirements changed as I got closer to the process. The annual reviews
> became a time to "nitpick" on what I had done. Early on I was told to work
> collaboratively in publishing; later I was told I should have had predomi-
> nantly single-author pieces. [Patitu, 2002, raw data]

Tamara, in her third year of service and so still involved in the tenure process, also was not happy. In particular, she did not like the unwritten rules.

> It has been my experience that there are a lot of "unwritten" rules about a
> tenure-track position. Collegiality and citizenship, whether universities want
> to admit it or not, play a large role, in that some colleagues will either support

you or not, based on triviality, and not on your academic work. Some senior faculty like to say that the rules for tenure have not changed since they went through the process. I find this statement to be an insult to one's intelligence. The rules of the tenure game keep changing. As a faculty of color, I hoped and prayed that I had every "I" dotted and every "T" crossed while going through the process for promotion and tenure. I did not want to give my colleagues an opportunity to question anything in my dossier. I want to be tenured because the scholarly evidence was there, because I worked my tail off, and I deserved it. [Patitu, 2002, raw data]

Also experiencing frustration, Renee commented, "White males were not required to do the same amount of research" (Patitu, 2002, raw data).

According to the junior faculty in the study, mentoring is critical during the tenure process. Renee stated, however, that she had received no mentoring. She also worried that there were no senior faculty in the program with which she was affiliated. She perceived that she had received no direction, although she had sought advice and suggestions from faculty members at other institutions. Renee worried constantly that she was not publishing enough.

Tamara also sought mentoring and identified several mentors who had helped her.

I have been fortunate to have several mentors in my field of expertise and also a senior, White, female colleague who has been instrumental in providing me with open, honest, and constructive feedback. I seek their advice when necessary and made sure that when I was preparing to go up for tenure and promotion, for example, that they understood my research, my split appointment, and how my split appointment is crucial to my research agenda. [Patitu, 2002, raw data]

The tenure process issues that surfaced for these African American women included conflicting information, unwritten rules, lack of direction and mentoring, and nitpicking or triviality. These issues must be addressed, because dissatisfaction with the promotion and tenure processes is one reason for the decline in African American faculty (Tack and Patitu, 1992).

Institutional Climate. The climate at an institution also can affect a faculty member's satisfaction; climate is a particular concern for a faculty member of color at a predominantly white institution. When describing the climate for faculty of color at their institutions, respondents noted a lack of commitment to affirmative action, the presence of very few African Americans, and conservative attitudes and beliefs. Armetha stated, for example, "I get along with my colleagues but the climate here is that affirmative action is out and most positions are filled based on power of influence, not necessarily the best qualified or wanting to have a diverse faculty representation" [Patitu, 2002, raw data].

For support, the participants turned to church, the few African American organizations available, or family. Linda, who stated that overall the climate at her university felt positive, commented that her "social environment revolves around church and a few professional Black organizations." Tamara asserted, "There are little to no social outlets like the performing arts, . . . cultural events, and the opportunity to meet other professionals of the opposite sex." Tamara also commented on her family as a support system: "My father, mother, and brother are here, so I am fortunate to have them as a support network" (Patitu, 2002, raw data).

Salary. Salary was, at one time, thought to be an important factor in the job dissatisfaction of faculty, particularly faculty of color and women (Edmundson, 1969; Winkler, 1982). Therefore, the respondents were asked what concerns, if any, they had about their salaries. Armetha, the professor, and Renee, the new assistant professor, both felt that their salaries were comparable to those of other faculty. However, Linda, the associate professor, and Tamara, the other assistant professor up for tenure and promotion, felt strongly that their salaries were not comparable to those of their colleagues, especially the men. Linda commented, "My impression is that my male colleagues have a higher salary than I do. The one thing I've learned is how important it is to negotiate your salary upfront." Tamara stated:

> From listening to senior, White, female colleagues in my department, I am sure that my salary is not comparable. I am concerned that salary often detracts from attracting senior faculty of color to the university. The university has a tendency to be stringent about not hiring someone at a higher salary level than what we offer a current faculty member. Yet, other institutions do this all the time. The system is not perfect and equal, it never has been. [Patitu, 2002, raw data]

Discussion

Myers (2002) asserts, "African American women live in a society that devalues both their sex and their race" (p. 6). The African American women in these studies have experienced overt and covert racism, sexism, and homophobia. They have been devalued, excluded, marginalized or mistreated because of who they are. Those who aspire to be tenured believe they are less likely to receive mentoring and direction on their pursuits than white faculty. Furthermore, they believe they are less likely to be asked to coauthor a publication by a senior white faculty member.

When it is time for them to go up for tenure, they assert, the rules change. And one of the subjects stated, "White males were not required to do the same amount of research." These respondents feel that expectations are higher for them than for white or male colleagues. Worse yet, they are working solo with their feelings of loneliness and isolation, in hostile environments with a lack of support. They also feel they have to try to fit in and repeatedly prove that they can do the job as they are constantly watched. And worse yet, these respondents do not believe their institutions are committed to diversity, and they feel the institutional climates are not good for them. On top of all of this, they feel their salaries are not comparable with their colleagues, especially the men.

These issues have surfaced over the years for these respondents. This leads us to conclude that little has changed for these African American women and to speculate that little has changed for African American female faculty and administrators in general.

As we stated previously, in 2002 in Fall 1999 African American women held only 5 percent of the executive, administrative, and managerial staff positions in institutions of higher education (National Center for Education Statistics, 2002). Faculty are not reaching the full professor level, "a highly valued, powerful status in which people of color and women continue to be vastly underrepresented" (Allen and others, 2002, p. 190). African American women represent only 1 percent of all full professors in degree-granting institutions, and as previously stated, African American women represent only 2.5 percent of the full-time instructional faculty in degree-granting institutions (National Center for Education Statistics, 2002). Their low numbers in turn make it harder to recruit other African American faculty, administrators, staff, and students.

Institutions must act to increase and retain African American women in higher education. Colleges and universities must value a diverse workforce in all branches of their institutions. These women have rich backgrounds and bring diversity in their experiences, their perspectives, and their abilities. They also bring different worldviews, which help to promote a multicultural environment. Furthermore, their presence is crucial for the personal and academic success of minority students for whom they act as mentors, role models, and advisers and for white students, who need the opportunity to interact with African American faculty to overcome misconceptions about the intellectual capabilities of minorities, especially African Americans. A diverse faculty and curriculum, which these women help to create, "enriches students' overall education by allowing them to experience people and ideas that they are likely to encounter as they move further away from their localized comfort zone and into our increasingly heterogeneous society." (Jimoh and Johnson, 2002, p. 288).

Their presence also is crucial for white faculty, who need to interact with African American faculty to gain a better understanding of minority cultures. In addition, African American women faculty are involved in research and development that bring in different perspectives, and they can serve as role models in the research arena for their minority colleagues. And they need each other for their survival. Serious steps must be taken by predominantly white institutions to address the serious issues that African American females face in higher education, in order to ensure a welcoming environment conducive to their success.

Recommendations

Although the studies described here examined the experiences of only five faculty members and five administrators, it still is possible to identify steps that PWIs might take to attract, hire, develop, and retain African American women administrators and faculty. First, Sagaria (2002) suggests these institutions "must provide leadership and resources to improve search processes" (p. 705) by educating search committees to reveal unconscious and subconscious institutional and individual biases; use a follow-up interview for candidates who did not receive an offer or who turned down the position, to determine how the institution could become more effective in recruiting and hiring African American women administrators and faculty; and hold senior administrators "accountable for the behavior of search committees and the outcomes of the searches" (p. 705).

Also, PWIs should consider ongoing assessments to determine whether discrimination based on race, gender, and sexual orientation persists. This can be accomplished by cultural audits of each academic and administrative unit on campus.

When recruiting faculty and administrators, PWIs should emphasize the opportunities and support systems available for research and teaching. Mentoring also should be provided by individuals who are sensitive to the problems faced by women of color.

Also, African American women should be assisted in establishing contacts within the African American community. Doing so relieves some of the isolation that often is felt by African American faculty and administrators new to an institution. For the same reasons, institutions should avoid having only one African American faculty member or administrator in a department. As Renee, a faculty member in one of the studies, said:

> Many times, people of color are the sole entity or voice in a department. This sort of lone wolf environment breeds an atmosphere that may further marginalize the person of color. Persons of color should not be forced into situations where they are the representative from the race; this is often the case at many institutions. [Patitu, 2002, raw data]

To help African American women alleviate the isolation and loneliness that they experience on their campuses, support systems should be established. An example of a support system is the Women of Color in the Academy Project (WOCAP) at the Center for the Education of Women, University of Michigan (2003), which "grew out of discussions with women of color faculty who expressed their concerns that there needed to be extended, focused attention to issues pertaining to women of color and students." The Office of the Provost currently supports the project, which is administered through the Center for the Education of Women. The purposes of WOCAP include the following:

1. To highlight the contributions that women of color make to the University community and to society at large, both academically and culturally; and

2. To build a network of women of color faculty that serves as a support system for research undertakings, academic career development, and enhanced career satisfaction, thus supporting their retention. [Center for the Education of Women, University of Michigan, 2003]

Predominantly white institutions also must provide and encourage supportive professional networks on and off campus to help African American female administrators and faculty feel included, valued, and respected and to help them with their academic career development, especially knowing "the informal networks of friendship and collegial exchange that silently influence the promotion and tenure review remain largely unavailable to women" (Kolodny, 2002, p. 90).

Because it is possible that African American female administrators and faculty feel they face hostile environments, prejudice, racism, and sexism in their work environments, PWIs should require diversity training for all faculty and administrators. Individuals must learn to appreciate the contributions of African American women and other minority groups and to celebrate their differences. Many groups provide diversity training, including the National Coalition Building Institute (NCBI), which works to eliminate prejudice and intergroup conflict in communities throughout the world. NCBI has conducted effective diversity programs on hundreds of college campuses and has campus affiliates at sixty-five colleges and universities in the United States and Canada (National Coalition Building Institute, 2003). By changing the institutional ethos to value and exhibit multicultural competence, PWIs could improve the hiring and retention of African American women administrators and faculty (Hinton, 2001).

Institutions must also take serious action against those individuals who harass and illegally discriminate against African American women and other minority groups. There must be zero tolerance for harassment of persons of color. The attackers and their superiors who ignore their behavior must be held accountable. Too often the victims leave the environment, when the attackers should be the ones who are pushed out.

Finally, institutional evaluation processes should include a commitment to diversity. For example, are various perspectives and worldviews explored in the curriculum? Does programming include diverse speakers and diverse topics? What is the minority enrollment and retention for faculty staff and students within a given department? These and many other questions need to be asked as we evaluate the people and elements in institutions of higher education.

References

Allen, W., Epps, E., Guillory, E., Suh, S., Bonous-Hammarth, M., and Stassen, M. "Outsiders Within: Race, Gender, and Faculty Status in U.S. Higher Education." In W. Smith, P. Altbach, and K. Lomotey (eds.), *The Racial Crisis in American Higher Education: Continuing Challenges for the Twenty-First Century*. Albany: State University of New York Press, 2002.

Center for the Education of Women, University of Michigan. "Women of Color in the Academy Project." [http://www.umich.edu/~cew/WOCAP.html]. Retrieved Aug. 19, 2003.

Collins, P. H. *Fighting Words: Black Women and the Search for Justice.* Minneapolis: University of Minnesota Press, 1998.

Delgado-Romero, E., Howard-Hamilton, M., and Vandiver, B. "Predictors of Burnout Among Faculty and Administrators Who Are People of Color." Unpublished manuscript, 2003.

Edmundson, J. *An Identification of Selected Items Associated with Faculty Job Satisfaction in the North Carolina System of Community Colleges.* Raleigh: North Carolina State University, 1969. (ED 045 940)

Fleming, J. *Blacks in College: A Comparative Study of Students' Success in Black and White Institutions.* San Francisco: Jossey-Bass, 1984.

Gardiner, M., Enomoto, E., and Grogan, M. *Coloring Outside the Lines: Mentoring Women in School Leadership.* Albany: State University of New York Press, 2000.

Gregory, S. T. "Black Faculty Women in the Academy: History, Status, and Future." *Journal of Negro Education,* 2001, *70,* 3.

Hinton, K. G. "The Experiences of African American Women Administrators at Predominantly White Institutions of Higher Education." Unpublished doctoral dissertation, Indiana University, 2001.

Jackson, J. F. "A New Test for Diversity: Retaining African American Administrators at Predominantly White Institutions." In L. Jones (ed.), *Retaining African Americans in Higher Education: Challenging Paradigms for Retaining Students, Faculty, and Administrators.* Sterling, Va.: Stylus, 2001.

James, J., and Farmer, R. (eds.). *Spirit, Space and Survival: African American Women in (White) Academe.* New York: Routledge, 1993.

Jimoh, A., and Johnson, C. "Racing into the Academcy: Pedagogy and Black Faculty." In B. Tusmith and M. Reddy (eds.), *Race in the College Classroom.* New Brunswick, N.J.: Rutgers University Press, 2002.

Kolodny, A. "Raising Standards While Lowering Anxieties: Rethinking the Promotion and Tenure Process." In S. G. Lim and M. Herrera-Sobek (eds.), *Power, Race, and Gender in Academe.* New York: Modern Language Association of America, 2002.

Mintz, B., and Rothblum, E. *Lesbians in Academia.* New York: Routledge, 1997.

Myers, L. *A Broken Silence: Voices of African American Women in the Academy.* Westport, Conn.: Bergin & Garvey, 2002.

National Center for Education Statistics. *Digest of Education Statistics.* Washington, D.C.: U.S. Department of Education, 2002.

National Coalition Building Institute. "About NCBI." [http://www.ncbi.org/aboutncbi]. Retrieved Aug. 19, 2003.

Noble, J. "The Higher Education of African American Women in the Twentieth Century." In J. Glazer, E. Bensimon, and B. Townsend, (eds.), *Women in Higher Education: A Feminist Perspective.* New York: Ginn Press, 1993.

Patitu, C. "The Experiences of African American Women Faculty in Higher Education." Unpublished raw data, 2002.

Patitu, C. L., and Tack, M. W. "Women and Faculty of Color: Higher Education's Most Endangered Resources." *NASPA Journal*, 1998, *1*(1), 7–25.

Rusher, A. *African American Women Administrators*. New York: University of America Press, 1996.

Sagaria, M. A. "An Exploratory Model of Filtering in Administrative Searches: Toward Counter-Hegemonic Discourses." *Journal of Higher Education*, 2002, *73*(6), 677–710.

Smith, A., and Stewart, A. "Approaches to Studying Racism and Sexism in African American Women's Lives." *Journal of Social Issues*, 1983, *39*(3), 1–15.

Tack, M., and Patitu, C. *Faculty Job Satisfaction: Women and Minorities in Peril*. ASHE-ERIC Higher Education Report no. 4. Washington, D.C.: School of Education and Human Development, George Washington University, 1992.

Winkler, L. "Job Satisfaction of University Faculty in the United States." Unpublished doctoral dissertation, University of Nebraska, 1982.

CAROL LOGAN PATITU is associate professor of student personnel administration in the Department of Educational Foundations at Buffalo State College in Buffalo, New York.

KANDACE G. HINTON is assistant professor of higher education leadership in the Department of Educational Leadership, Administration, and Foundations at Indiana State University in Terre Haute.

8

This chapter continues and expands the dialogue regarding the oppressions experienced by African American women in higher education. Stakeholders of postsecondary education are invited to use this dialogue to become more aware of the needs of African American women on college campuses, as well as African American people in general.

Insights: Emphasizing Issues That Affect African American Women

Robin L. Hughes, Mary F. Howard-Hamilton

The authors of the preceding chapters leave us with a perplexing and challenging question: Where do institutions of higher education, African American women, and other higher education stakeholders go from here to address the many obstacles faced by African American women in higher education? African American women enter institutions of higher education that are characterized by barriers constructed according to race, sex, and class. To feel a sense of connection with the majority culture on predominantly white campuses, African American women may find themselves assimilating, so that they can find support systems and not feel ostracized and isolated (Evans, Forney, and Guido-DiBrito, 1998). In this final chapter, the dialogue begun in the previous chapters continues but has been expanded to present additional concepts, policies, and interventions.

This chapter encourages institutions of higher education and all of their stakeholders (students, faculty, and staff) to be cognizant not only of the institutional environments for African American women but also of the experiences and needs of African American women in higher education.

Challenges: Context for the Dialogue

African American women on college campuses should not be placed into the one-size-fits-all framework of "black people," because it ignores the within-group differences that affect them. Not being attentive to these issues continues to exacerbate the problems African American women face on campus, thus stifling the dialogue that could empower and uplift them.

NEW DIRECTIONS FOR STUDENT SERVICES, no. 104, Winter 2003 © Wiley Periodicals, Inc.

Critical Mass. Each of the chapter authors notes the importance of having a critical mass of African women—faculty members, staff, and students—on campus. In this final chapter, we emphasize its importance by revealing some of the underlying challenges that African Americans face in higher education. Research from noted educational policy scholars reveals that the most important challenges that African Americans face in higher education are those of recruitment and retention. Critical mass is an important concept in recruiting and retaining African American students, faculty, and staff, as well as in alleviating some of the obstacles that African Americans face on college campuses.

According to Miller (2003), "critical mass is an underlying theme of affirmative action. However, the concept has been broadened in light of the case regarding affirmative action at the University of Michigan" (p. 1). According to the Regents of the University of Michigan, students from a wide range of backgrounds learn more from others who are unlike themselves (*Grutter v. Bollinger,* 2002). In order to realize this goal, schools should seek a critical mass of minority students to "ensure that all students—minority and majority alike—will be able to enjoy the educational benefits of an academically diverse student body" (*Grutter v. Bollinger,* 2002, p. 1).

A critical mass exists whenever there are enough individuals from a particular group that they feel comfortable participating in conversations and enough that other students see them as individuals rather than as spokespersons for their race (Miller, 2003).

Recruitment, Retention, and Affirmative Action. Research by Orfield (2000) reveals that changes in access of African Americans in higher education and their persistence in it have occurred as a result of educational political movements. For instance, the gains of the civil rights movement challenged the tradition of racial exclusion. In addition, the creation of financial aid programs provided a stepping stone to education for those students who were less affluent, and the War on Poverty encouraged the poor to attend college (Orfield, 2000). Each of these initiatives has greatly influenced access to higher education for African Americans.

Guinier (2001) and Springer and Baez (2002) emphasize that educational affirmative action policies benefit not only persons of color but all stakeholders in higher education. In fact, the intellectual and social development of minority and nonminority students can be enhanced by racial diversity on college campuses (Bok and Bowen, 1998; Guinier, 2001; American Psychological Association, 1999; Springer and Baez, 2002). For example, students exhibit deeper and more complex thinking, a greater likelihood of involvement in civic activities, a greater ability to understand new perspectives, and an enhanced interest in pursuing graduate work when engaged with diversity (Nora and Cabrera, 1996). In addition, white students who attend racially diverse institutions benefit by learning from and using diverse perspectives and by having nonwhite friends, and they perceive campuses that accept and respect black students as positive (Nora and Cabrera, 1996).

Paradoxically, scholars such as Clegg (2002) debate the merits of diversity and affirmative action. They argue that time alone has brought about educational changes for African American women and people of color, so there is little need for affirmative action policies. This same argument is also transmitted to broader audiences and stakeholders; for example, states such as Texas believe that they have fulfilled the obligation to remedy a history of overt discrimination and that it is neither necessary nor permissible to continue racially targeted efforts to raise minority enrollment in the state's public universities (Chapa and Lazardo, 2000, p. 51).

In states such as Texas where affirmative action policies have been struck down, there has been a significant decline in the number of African Americans who attend institutions of higher education and a subsequent decline in the number of African American professors and graduate students (Orfield, 2000).

In fact, as Orfield (2000) notes, current institutional demographics across the country reflect a perpetuation of the status quo. Although communities that surround institutions of higher education have become more diverse, college campuses that have been forced to end affirmative action policies are rapidly becoming less diverse (Orfield, 2000). For example, the percentage of doctoral degrees awarded to African American students remains virtually the same now as in 1986 (Hacker, 1992). In 1986, only 804 of the 22,984 doctoral recipients from all fields (3.5 percent) were African American (Hacker, 1992). Five years later, in 1991, although the total number of doctoral recipients increased by over 10 percent, African American doctoral recipients increased by only about 0.3 percent (Hacker, 1992). Ten years later, the *Chronicle of Higher Education Almanac* (2002) reported only a 1 percent increase from 1991 to 2000 in doctoral degrees awarded to African Americans. In fact, the number of African Americans receiving doctorates still is so small that if every one became a faculty member, this would have a negligible effect on the proportion of African Americans in the professoriate (Ladson-Billings, 1998).

The number of African American faculty members also has an impact on whether students are attracted and retained in institutions of higher education (Howard-Hamilton, Phelps, and Torres, 1998; Freeman, 1997; Hughes, 2001). In fact, the success of black students who attend predominantly white institutions (PWIs) is greatly influenced by relationships with faculty, administrators, and students (Howard-Hamilton, Phelps, and Torres, 1998; Freeman, 1997; Hughes, 2001). For example, according to Defour and Hirsch (1990), the sheer presence of African American faculty at institutions of higher education may encourage African American students to persist.

Indeed, a major source of frustration for African American students is the lack of African American role models in visible leadership positions

(Freeman, 1997; Hughes, forthcoming). There are also insufficient numbers and varieties of ethnic studies programs and relevant outside student activities for students of color (Freeman, 1997; Hughes, 2001).

Despite a clarion call from multiple stakeholders at institutions of higher education to increase the number of African American faculty on college campuses, the current figures reveal that shortages continue throughout the academy. In 2002, African Americans were only 4.5 percent of the professoriate (*Chronicle of Higher Education Almanac*, 2002). Even that small figure is deceptive. Blacks compose approximately 1 percent of the faculty employed by predominantly white colleges and universities; the other 3.5 percent are employed by historically black colleges and universities (*Chronicle of Higher Education Almanac*, 2002).

The number of African American women on college campuses is also critically important for retention and success of black women students, faculty, and staff (Myers, 2002). The number of African American women on campus is important in sharing ideas and concerns that may be common to African American women. African American women report that working at campuses where there is a critical mass of African women is less stressful than at those without a critical mass. This feeling is similar to that reported by most new faculty and by faculty women in general; however, the experiences of African American women are embedded in racism as well as sexism.

In addition, the number of African American women on college campuses is relatively small. For example, women constitute 27.3 percent of all faculty members in institutions of higher education. However, African American women represent only 2.2 percent of full-time faculty at institutions of higher education (Gregory, 1999).

The number of African American women in senior leadership positions in higher education also is small. About 6 percent, or 136, of the senior administrative leadership positions in institutions of higher education are held by African Americans (American Council on Education, 2000). In 2000, only 50 of those 136 senior leaders were African American women (American Council on Education, 2000).

Given these figures, it is clear that universities and departments that take a generic approach to assist African American women will do little to combat the pervasive isolation and stress that result from the lack of a critical mass of African Americans and African American women (Myers, 2002; hooks, 1999). Effective strategies to promote the success of African American women in higher education are addressed in the rest of this chapter.

Summarizing the Dialogue

The most salient theme across the chapters of this sourcebook is that African American women experience psychological and physical tolls as a result of the obstacles they face on college campuses. Each of the authors in the sourcebook stated that these obstacles perpetuate difficulties in recruiting and retaining the essential critical mass of African American faculty, staff, and students.

Obstacle: Systemic Racism. Systemic racism is perhaps the most serious obstacle faced by African American women in higher education. The chapters in this volume provide evidence that racial and gender inequality continue to be prevalent in American higher education. Forms of de facto segregation have lingering social, physical, and psychological effects and can become embedded in campus academic and political systems in both overt and covert ways (Ladson-Billings, 1998). One example of de facto segregation is the selection of persons for key administrative or faculty roles who mirror the majority group on campus. Other forms include students of color choosing to segregate themselves by living in residential areas that have a high proportion of racial and ethnic minorities and by communing together in dining facilities. Many campuses have cultural centers that allow students of color to find a space in which they feel at home, but many majority-group students are uncomfortable venturing into these places. The chapters in this volume also illustrate the point that, although we are in the twenty-first century, many campus practices are similar to those experienced by students who attended college in the post–civil rights era. Systemic campus racism rears its ugly head when, for example, activities such as slave auctions or ghetto parties held by predominantly white organizations are still conducted and condoned on campuses across the country.

Examples of systemic racism described by the authors in this sourcebook include the assumption that high-achieving African American professors are exceptional and the subtle innuendos of incompetence and inexperience expressed when the leader of a unit is an African American woman. Evidence of systemic racism also can be found in the classroom when students question, query, challenge, and dismiss the intellectual ability of an African American faculty member. In all of these situations, no amount of experience is enough to prove that she is highly capable when the group comprises people who do not look like her.

The chapters in this sourcebook also illustrate that black women often are treated as second-class citizens who must meet different demands and expectations from their white counterparts. For example, Patitu and Hinton (Chapter Seven) note that the faculty women in Patitu's study felt they were expected to do more work, with fewer rewards, than their white male colleagues. In addition, unlike their white colleagues, African American women frequently are sought out by students of color who are looking for a familiar face, camaraderie, an advocate, or an adviser. This places a significant amount of stress on faculty members.

Obstacle: Small Numbers. In Chapter One, Zamani notes that African American women are present in institutions of higher education in greater numbers than their male counterparts. Research described in this sourcebook reiterates, however, that a very small number of African American faculty and staff are present in PWIs, another obstacle to effectiveness and success. Small numbers mean additional responsibilities for working with African American students as well as white students, and increased requests for institutional service. For example, Zamani (Chapter One) notes that although African American women comprise about 8 percent of the undergraduate population, the number of African American women faculty members on campuses is about 2.2 percent (Gregory, 1999). Because African American students are likely to seek African American role models, the role models experience significant demands to spend time with African American students.

These demands come in addition to the typical pressures to teach, research, and publish faced by all faculty. For instance, several authors in this volume noted that African American female administrators and faculty state that they are more involved in service, teaching, advising, and committee service than some of their white counterparts. They also noted that excessive participation in all of the activities required of faculty in addition to working with African American students can have serious professional and personal consequences.

In Chapters Three and Seven, Watt and Partitu and Hinton noted that African American women—faculty, administrators, and students—also are isolated in institutions of higher education. This isolation can lead to stress when it is coupled with internalization of regular oppression and microaggressions (see Chapter Two). Isolation also can lead African American women to feel insecure in their ability to compete with others on campus because they feel voiceless and invisible. Moreover, isolation and racism breed a lack of trust; to whom can an African American woman turn if she sees no professor or administrator who believes in her abilities and no support group to encourage her?

The most deleterious effect of isolation is burnout. Feelings of burnout can result in an individual leaving academe, never returning to higher education, and harboring ill will and resentment toward the institution for lack of support (Howard-Hamilton and Delgado-Romero, 2002).

Other authors comment that black women often are perceived as strong and independent and often feel they have to conform to this perception. But black women have been forced into this role because of inadequate support systems and isolation. Playing the role is stressful and takes a toll on all aspects of African American women's lives.

Perhaps most crucial of all the messages in this sourcebook is that African American women in higher education live at the intersection of two forms of oppression: racism and sexism. Dual oppression is problematic for many reasons. First, because gendered racism can be felt and understood only by those who are immersed in it, the experiences of African American women may be inaccessible to other women and to men of color, which further isolates African American women (St. Jean and Feagin, 1998). St. Jean and Feagin (1998) continue: "While solidarity with supportive white women can help alleviate some effects of gendered racism, black and white women are often adversaries" (p. 207).

Yet although white or male administrators and faculty cannot actually walk in the shoes of African American women, gaining knowledge about their experiences can facilitate dialogue that could, in turn, transform the campus community.

Dialogue and transformation are the goal of this sourcebook. In each chapter, the authors provide administrators, faculty, students, and—most important—African American women with salient points that provide guidelines for success and survival on college campuses. Recommendations based on those points follow.

Rising to the Challenge

So how do African American women share their plight and find ways to navigate the oppression they experience on campuses? First, a paradigm shift is needed to understand the impact of the layered dimensions of race and gender. The convergence of these forms of oppression can lead to duress that can only be experienced by African American women and is invisible to the dominant group on campus.

In Chapter Six, Patton and Harper assert that the most important step for institutions that wish to prove they are sincere about wanting to retain African American women, be they faculty, administrators, or students, is to provide support systems. Support systems include opportunities for African American women to form sister circles and share counterstories that refute some of the negative information they may have received during their daily campus routines. Such support systems are not intended to portray or reinforce a debilitating sense of self and hopelessness but, instead, provide settings in which to create an identity not based on gender roles or racial stereotyping. The role models and facilitators of these support groups should be African American women.

In Chapter Three, Watt emphasizes that African American women must provide spiritual and psychological support for one another. In a similar vein, bell hooks (1999) called for African American women "to stir from our psychic slumbers, to rise and rescue ourselves and one another" (p. 236). It is difficult, however, to find this type of spiritual bonding among African American women because of the environmental isolation that occurs when there are so few on campus and they are dispersed in so many places. On most campuses, contact is difficult and random. More effort and energy should be given to creating these connections.

One way that African American women can support one another is mentoring. The importance of the mentoring relationship is discussed extensively by Patton and Harper in Chapter Six, as well as by authors elsewhere (Hughes, 2001; Williams, 2001; Woods, 2001). These authors have listened to the voices of undergraduate and graduate African American women who have attempted to make a connection with their white advisers or faculty members and were rebuffed. In addition, because of the scarcity of women of color in faculty or administrative roles at predominantly white institutions,

African American women are likely to attempt to connect with women of color outside of their academic area. Overall, African American women students, faculty, and administrators on college campuses face daily challenges in their attempts to connect with one another. A mechanism to make this process more fluid and less cumbersome, such as a structured mentoring program facilitated by a highly visible office at the university, could make the mentor-protégée association less daunting.

All colleges and universities have the ability to develop activities, programming, and forms of scholarship in which students and faculty can become involved. In fact, many institutional mission statements present diversity initiatives as critical components of the campus ethos. Often these statements become so prevalent that they no longer are noticed, another form of de facto segregation. Therefore, all members of the institution have a responsibility to try to be aware of all aspects of the campus environment and ensure that all aspects are consistent with the ethos of the university.

Examples of such efforts include the creation and support of curricula that focus on multiculturalism and diversity issues, as well as faculty members who model teaching methods sensitive to the needs of students of color and teach majority students about the importance of cross-cultural interaction. This ethos also can be confirmed by campus activities that are inclusive and not solely geared toward dominant-group preferences; policy statements that clearly indicate penalties for hate crimes and incidents on campus; and the affirmation of faculty and administrators with promotion, tenure, and other recognition for their dedication to the enhancement of a multicultural environment on campus.

Ensuring Change

The growing number of students of color in higher education has caused many administrators and faculty to evaluate their multicultural competence. This sourcebook urges all members of the higher education community to examine their assumptions, attitudes, and effectiveness in dealing with the multiplicity of identities, values, mores and cultures presented by one group: African American women. African American women should receive intellectual, spiritual, psychological, and programmatic encouragement from everyone on the campus, as noted in Chapters Four and Five.

Responsibility for providing supportive environments for African American women should not be left to women of color only; the entire community should be engaged in making sure that black women's road to access and success is negotiable. "Black women in the academy differ in their experiences, backgrounds, appearances, educational levels, demographics, occupations, and beliefs. What connects them all is the struggle to be accepted and respected members of society and their desire to have a voice that can be heard in a world with many views" (Collins, 2001, p. 39). Changes necessary to create these environments and opportunities must be initiated and embraced by individuals who have the power and authority to move the campus toward cultural enlightenment.

Change also can happen in small ways at individual levels. As an administrator or faculty member, reflect on the last conversation or substantive contact you had with an African American woman student on your campus. What did you learn? What issues did she present that were new or different from your point of view? How will you use these perspectives to challenge others to become more understanding and supportive of these women? If you have not had a conversation with an African American woman or a group of African American women, why has this not occurred? Could it be that there are so few that they have become virtually invisible? If so, is this invisibility a choice of the women, or is it a result of the lack of receptivity of the institution to the voices of African American women?

Implementing the suggestions provided throughout this sourcebook can be challenging, but if we are posturing for change, it is time to take action. The African American women in the academy await your response.

References

American Council on Education. *Annual Status Report Minorities in Higher Education.* Washington, D.C.: American Council on Higher Education, 2000.

American Psychological Association. *How Affirmative Action Benefits America.* Washington, D.C.: Office of Public Communication, 1999. (Brochure)

Bok, D., and Bowen, W. *The Shape of the River: Long-Term Consequences of Considering Race in College and University Admissions.* Princeton, N.J.: Princeton University Press, 1998.

Chapa, J., and Lazardo, V. "Hopwood in Texas: The Untimely End of Affirmative Action." In G. Orfield and E. Miller (eds.), *Chilling Admissions: The Affirmative Action Crisis and the Search for Alternatives.* Cambridge, Mass.: Harvard Education Publishing Group, 2000.

Chronicle of Higher Education Almanac. "Characteristics of Faculty Members with Teaching Duties by Type of Institution." [http://chronicle.com/weekly/almanac/2002/nation/0103102.htm]. Retrieved Aug. 10, 2002.

Clegg, R. "When Faculty Hiring Is Blatantly Illegal." *Chronicle of Higher Education,* Nov. 1, 2002.

Collins, A. C. "Black Women in the Academy: An Historical Overview." In R. O. Mabokela and A. L. Green (eds.), *Sisters of the Academy: Emergent Black Women Scholars in Higher Education.* Sterling, Va.: Stylus, 2001.

Defour, D., and Hirsch, B. "The Adaptation of Black Graduate Students: A Social Network Approach." *American Journal of Social Psychology,* 1990, *18,* 487–503.

Evans, N., Forney, D., and Guido-DiBrito, F. *Student Development in College: Theory, Research, and Practice.* San Francisco: Jossey-Bass, 1998.

Freeman, K. "Increasing African Americans' Participation in Higher Education: African American High-School Students' Perspective." *Journal of Higher Education,* 1997, *68*(5), 523–550.

Gregory, S. *Black Women in the Academy: The Secrets to Success and Achievement.* New York: University Press of America, 1999.

Grutter v. Bollinger, et al. United States Court of Appeals for the Sixth Cirtuit. Nos. 01–1447/1516. 2002. [http://www.umich.edu/~urel/admissions/legal/grutter/gru-ap-op.html].

Guinier, L. "Colleges Should Take Confirmative Action in Admissions." *Chronicle of Higher Education,* Dec. 14, 2001, B10–B12.

Hacker, A. *Two Nations: Black and White, Separate, Hostile, and Unequal.* New York: Scribner, 1992.

hooks, b. *Remembered Rapture.* New York: Henry Holt, 1999.

Howard-Hamilton, M. F., and Delgado-Romero, E. *The Relationship Among Workload, Burnout, and Stress of Full-Time Faculty and Administrators Who Are People of Color.* Washington, D.C.: NASPA Center for Scholarship, Research, and Professional Development for Women, 2002.

Howard-Hamilton, M. F., Phelps, R. E., and Torres, V. "Meeting the Needs of All Students and Staff Members: The Challenge of Diversity." In D. L. Cooper and J. M. Lancaster (eds.), *Beyond Law and Policy: Reaffirming the Role of Student Affairs.* New Directions for Student Services, no. 82. San Francisco: Jossey-Bass, 1998.

Hughes, R. "Student Development and Change: Student and Parent Expectations and Experience." Unpublished doctoral dissertation, Texas A&M University, College Station, Texas, 2001.

Hughes, R. "The Dwindling Pool of Qualified Professors of Color: Suburban Legends." In D. Cleveland (ed.), *A Long Way to Go: Conversations About Race by African American Faculty and Students on the Journey to the Professorate.* New York: Peter Lang, forthcoming.

Ladson-Billings, G. "Just What Is Critical Race Theory and What's It Doing in a Nice Field Like Education?" *Qualitative Studies in Education,* 1998, *11*(1), 7–24.

Miller, C. "The Controversy in Achieving Critical Mass." [http://journalism.medill.northwestern.edu/docket/02–0516criticalmass.html]. Retrieved Sept. 7, 2003.

Myers, L. W. *A Broken Silence: Voices of African American Women in the Academy.* Westport, Conn.: Bergin & Garvey, 2002.

Nora A., and Cabrera, A. "The Role of Perception of Prejudice and Discrimination on the Adjustment of Minority Students to College." *Journal of Higher Education,* 1996, *67*(2), 119–148.

Orfield, G. "Campus Resegregation and Its Alternatives." In G. Orfield and E. Miller (eds.), *Chilling Admissions: The Affirmative Action Crisis and the Search for Alternatives.* Cambridge, Mass.: Harvard Education Publishing Group, 2000.

Springer, A., and Baez, B. "Affirmative Action Is Not Discrimination." *Chronicle of Higher Education,* 2002, *49*(15), B17.

St. Jean, Y., and Feagin, J. R. *Double Burden: Black Women and Everyday Racism.* New York: Sharpe, 1998.

Williams, L. D. "Coming to Terms with Being a Young, Black Female Academic in U.S. Higher Education." In R. O. Mabokela and A. L. Green (eds.), *Sisters of the Academy: Emergent Black Women Scholars in Higher Education.* Sterling, Va.: Stylus, 2001.

Woods, R. L. "Invisible Women: The Experiences of Black Female Doctoral Students at the University of Michigan." In R. O. Mabokela and A. L. Green (eds.), *Sisters of the Academy: Emergent Black Women Scholars in Higher Education.* Sterling, Va.: Stylus, 2001.

ROBIN L. HUGHES *is assistant professor in the School of Education at Oklahoma State University in Stillwater.*

MARY F. HOWARD-HAMILTON *is associate dean of graduate studies and associate professor in the Department of Educational Leadership and Policy Studies, Higher Education and Student Affairs Program, at the W. W. Wright School of Education, Indiana University–Bloomington.*

INDEX

Back Issue/Subscription Order Form

Copy or detach and send to:
Jossey-Bass, A Wiley Imprint, 989 Market Street, San Francisco CA 94103-1741

Call or fax toll-free: Phone 888-378-2537 6:30AM – 3PM PST; Fax 888-481-2665

Back Issues: Please send me the following issues at $27 each
(Important: please include ISBN number with your order.)

_____

_____

_____

$ _____   Total for single issues

$ _____   SHIPPING CHARGES: SURFACE   Domestic   Canadian

	First Item	$5.00	$6.00
	Each Add'l Item	$3.00	$1.50

For next-day and second-day delivery rates, call the number listed above.

Subscriptions   Please __ start __ renew my subscription to *New Directions for Student Services* for the year 2_____ at the following rate:

U.S.	__ Individual $75	__ Institutional $160
Canada	__ Individual $75	__ Institutional $200
All Others	__ Individual $99	__ Institutional $234
Online Subscription		__ Institutional $160

**For more information about online subscriptions visit
www.interscience.wiley.com**

$ _____   Total single issues and subscriptions (Add appropriate sales tax for your state for single issue orders. No sales tax for U.S. subscriptions. Canadian residents, add GST for subscriptions and single issues.)

__Payment enclosed (U.S. check or money order only)
__VISA __ MC __ AmEx __ Card #_____ Exp.Date_____

Signature _____ Day Phone _____
__Bill Me (U.S. institutional orders only. Purchase order required.)

Purchase order # _____
       Federal Tax ID13559302   **GST 89102 8052**

Name _____

Address _____

_____

Phone _____ E-mail _____

For more information about Jossey-Bass, visit our Web site at www.josseybass.com

SS103   Contemporary Financial Issues in Student Affairs
John H. Schuh
This volume addresses the challenging financial situation facing higher
education and offers creative solutions for student affairs staff. Topics
include the differences between public and private institutions in funding
student activities, how to demonstrate financial accountability to
stakeholders, plus ways to address budget challenges in student unions,
health centers, campus recreation, counseling centers, and student housing.
ISBN: 0-7879-7173-1

SS102   Meeting the Special Needs of Adult Students
Deborah Kilgore, Penny J. Rice
This volume examines the ways student services professionals can best help
adult learners. Chapters highlight the specific challenges that adult
enrollment brings to traditional four-year and postgraduate institutions,
which are often focused on the traditional-aged student experience.
Explaining that adult students are typically involved in campus life in
different ways than younger students are, the volume provides student
services professionals with good guidance on serving an ever-growing
population.
ISBN: 0-7879-6991-5

SS101   Planning and Achieving Successful Student Affairs Facilities Projects
Jerry Price
Provides student affairs professionals with an examination of critical
facilities issues by exploring the experiences of their colleagues. Illustrates
that students' educational experiences are affected by residence halls,
student unions, dining services, recreation and wellness centers, and campus
grounds, and that student affairs professionals make valuable contributions
to the success of campus facility projects. Covers planning, budgeting,
collaboration, and communication through case studies and lessons learned.
ISBN: 0-7879-6847-1

SS100   Student Affairs and External Relations
Mary Beth Snyder
Building positive relations with external constituents is as important in
student affairs work as it is in any other university or college division. This
issue is a long-overdue resource of ideas, strategies, and information aimed
at making student affairs leaders more effective in their interactions with
important off-campus partners, supporters, and agencies. Chapter authors
explore the current challenges facing the student services profession as well
as the emerging opportunities worthy of student affairs interest.
ISBN: 0-7879-6342-9

SS99   Addressing Contemporary Campus Safety Issues
Christine K. Wilkinson, James A. Rund
Provided for practitioners as a resource book for both historical and evolving
issues, this guide covers hazing, parental partnerships, and collaborative

relationships between universities and the neighboring community. Addressing a new definition of a safe campus environment, the editors have identified topics such as the growth in study abroad, the implications of increased usage of technology on campus, and campus response to September 11. In addition, large-scale crisis responses to student riots and multiple campus tragedies have been described in case studies. The issue speaks to a more contemporary definition of a safe campus environment that addresses not only physical safety issues but also those of a psychological nature, a more diverse student body, and quality of life.
ISBN: 0-7879-6341-0

SS98   **The Art and Practical Wisdom of Student Affairs Leadership**
Jon Dalton, Marguerite McClinton
This issue collects reflections, stories, and advice about the art and practice of student affairs leadership. Ten senior student affairs leaders were asked to maintain a journal and record their personal reflections on practical wisdom they have gained in the profession. The authors looked inside themselves to provide personal and candid insight into the convictions and values that have guided them in their work and lives.
ISBN: 0-7879-6340-2

SS97   **Working with Asian American College Students**
Marylu K. McEwen, Corinne Maekawa Kodama, Alvin N. Alvarez, Sunny Lee, Christopher T. H. Liang
Highlights the diversity of Asian American college students, analyzes the "model minority" myth and the stereotype of the "perfidious foreigner," and points out the need to consider the racial identity and racial consciousness of Asian American students. Various authors propose a model of Asian American student development, address issues of Asian Americans who are at educational risk, discuss the importance of integration and collaboration between student affairs and Asian American studies programs, and offer strategies for developing socially conscious Asian American student leaders.
ISBN: 0-7879-6292-9S

SS96   **Developing External Partnerships for Cost-Effective, Enhanced Service**
Larry H. Dietz, Ernest J. Enchelmayer
Offers a variety of models for the enhancement of services through external partnership, including on- and off-campus collaboration with public and private entities. Explores the challenges student affairs professionals face when determining how to meet a particular constituency's needs in the most cost-effective and efficient manner.
ISBN: 0-7879-5788-7

SS95   **The Implications of Student Spirituality for Student Affairs Practice**
Margaret A. Jablonski
Provides student affairs professionals and others on college campuses with information and guidance about including spirituality in student life programs and in the curriculum of preparation programs. Explores the role that faith and spirit play in individual and group development on our campuses. Models of leadership, staff development, and graduate education itself are all examined from the context of spirituality.
ISBN: 0-7879-5787-9

SS94   **Consumers, Adversaries, and Partners: Working with the Families of Undergraduates**
Bonnie V. Daniel, B. Ross Scott
Presents effective strategies for student services professionals to collaborate and coordinate in creating a consistent message of engagement for the families of today's college students. Parents, stepparents, grandparents, and others who serve as guardians of college students are challenging administrators to address their concerns in a variety of areas, including admissions and financial aid processes, orientation programs, residence life, and alumni and development activities.
ISBN: 0-7879-5786-0

SS93   **Student Services for Athletes**
Mary F. Howard-Hamilton, Sherry K. Watt
Explores a full range of issues, including the ongoing impact of Title IX, the integration of student athletes into on-campus residence halls, the college experience for minority athletes, and the expansion of opportunities for women athletes.
ISBN: 0-7879-5757-7

SS92   **Leadership and Management Issues for a New Century**
Dudley B. Woodard Jr., Patrick Love, Susan R. Komives
Examines new approaches to learning requiring a new kind of leadership, and describes the important role played by student affairs professionals in creating and sustaining learning communities. Explores how changes in students will affect student affairs work, outlines new dimensions of student affairs capital, and details the importance of active and collaborative leadership for creating a more flexible structure to handle future challenges.
ISBN: 0-7879-5445-4

SS91   **Serving Students with Disabilities**
Holley A. Belch
Explores the critical role that community and dignity play in creating a meaningful educational experience for students with disabilities and shows how to help these students gain meaningful access and full participation in campus activities. Addresses such common concerns as fulfilling legal requirements and overcoming architectural barriers, as well as effective approaches to recruitment and retention, strategies for career and academic advising, and the impact of financial resources on funding programs and services.
ISBN: 0-7879-5444-6

SS90   **Powerful Programming for Student Learning: Approaches That Make a Difference**
Debora L. Liddell, Jon P. Lund
Assists student affairs professionals as they plan, implement, and evaluate their educational interventions on college and university campuses. Details each step of program assessment, planning, implementation, and outcome evaluation. Explains the importance of collaborating with faculty and others, illustrating several types of programming partnerships with four brief case studies, and examines the significant partnership aspects that led to programming success.
ISBN: 0-7879-5443-8

NEW DIRECTIONS FOR STUDENT SERVICES IS NOW AVAILABLE ONLINE AT WILEY INTERSCIENCE

What is Wiley InterScience?

Wiley InterScience is the dynamic online content service from John Wiley & Sons delivering the full text of over 300 leading scientific, technical, medical, and professional journals, plus major reference works, the acclaimed *Current Protocols* laboratory manuals, and even the full text of select Wiley print books online.

What are some special features of Wiley InterScience?

Wiley InterScience Alerts is a service that delivers table of contents via e-mail for any journal available on Wiley InterScience as soon as a new issue is published online.
Early View is Wiley's exclusive service presenting individual articles online as soon as they are ready, even before the release of the compiled print issue. These articles are complete, peer-reviewed, and citable.
CrossRef is the innovative multi-publisher reference linking system enabling readers to move seamlessly from a reference in a journal article to the cited publication, typically located on a different server and published by a different publisher.

How can I access Wiley InterScience?

Visit http://www.interscience.wiley.com

Guest Users can browse Wiley InterScience for unrestricted access to journal Tables of Contents and Article Abstracts, or use the powerful search engine.
Registered Users are provided with a *Personal Home Page* to store and manage customized alerts, searches, and links to favorite journals and articles. Additionally, Registered Users can view free Online Sample Issues and preview selected material from major reference works.
Licensed Customers are entitled to access full-text journal articles in PDF, with select journals also offering full-text HTML.

How do I become an Authorized User?

Authorized Users are individuals authorized by a paying Customer to have access to the journals in Wiley InterScience. For example, a university that subscribes to Wiley journals is considered to be the Customer. Faculty, staff and students authorized by the university to have access to those journals in Wiley InterScience are Authorized Users. Users should contact their Library for information on which Wiley journals they have access to in Wiley InterScience.

ASK YOUR INSTITUTION ABOUT WILEY INTERSCIENCE TODAY!

United States Postal Service

Statement of Ownership, Management, and Circulation

1. Publication Title	2. Publication Number	3. Filing Date
New Directions For Student Services	0 1 6 4 - 7 9 7 0	9/30/03

4. Issue Frequency	5. Number of Issues Published Annually	6. Annual Subscription Price
Quarterly	4	$75 Individual $160 Institution

7. Complete Mailing Address of Known Office of Publication (Not printer) (Street, city, county, state, and ZIP+4)
989 Market Street
San Francisco, CA 94103-1741
San Francisco County

Contact Person
Joe Schuman
Telephone
415 782 3232

8. Complete Mailing Address of Headquarters or General Business Office of Publisher (Not printer)
Same as above

9. Full Names and Complete Mailing Addresses of Publisher, Editor, and Managing Editor (Do not leave blank)

Publisher (Name and complete mailing address)
Wiley, San Francisco
Jossey-Bass - Pfeiffer
Address - same as above

Editor (Name and complete mailing address)
John H. Schuh
N243 Lagomarcino Hall
Iowa State University
Ames, IA 50011

Managing Editor (Name and complete mailing address)
None

10. Owner (Do not leave blank. If the publication is owned by a corporation, give the name and address of the corporation immediately followed by the names and addresses of all stockholders owning or holding 1 percent or more of the total amount of stock. If not owned by a corporation, give the names and addresses of the individual owners. If owned by a partnership or other unincorporated firm, give its name and address as well as those of each individual owner. If the publication is published by a nonprofit organization, give its name and address.)

Full Name	Complete Mailing Address
John Wiley & Sons Inc.	111 River Street Hoboken, NJ 07030

11. Known Bondholders, Mortgagees, and Other Security Holders Owning or Holding 1 Percent or More of Total Amount of Bonds, Mortgages, or Other Securities. If none, check box ► ☐ None

Full Name	Complete Mailing Address
Same as above	Same as above

12. Tax Status (For completion by nonprofit organizations authorized to mail at nonprofit rates) (Check one)
The purpose, function, and nonprofit status of this organization and the exempt status for federal income tax purposes:
☐ Has Not Changed During Preceding 12 Months
☐ Has Changed During Preceding 12 Months (Publisher must submit explanation of change with this statement)

PS Form 3526, October 1999 (See Instructions on Reverse)

---

13. Publication Title	14. Issue Date for Circulation Data Below
New Directions For Student Services	Summer 2003

15.	Extent and Nature of Circulation	Average No. Copies Each Issue During Preceding 12 Months	No. Copies of Single Issue Published Nearest to Filing Date
a.	Total Number of Copies (Net press run)	1,493	1,505
b. Paid and/or Requested Circulation	(1) Paid/Requested Outside-County Mail Subscriptions Stated on Form 3541. (Include advertiser's proof and exchange copies)	609	616
	(2) Paid In-County Subscriptions Stated on Form 3541 (Include advertiser's proof and exchange copies)	0	0
	(3) Sales Through Dealers and Carriers, Street Vendors, Counter Sales, and Other Non-USPS Paid Distribution	0	0
	(4) Other Classes Mailed Through the USPS	0	0
c.	Total Paid and/or Requested Circulation (Sum of 15b. (1), (2),(3),and (4)) ►	609	616
d. Free Distribution by Mail (Samples, compliment ary, and other free)	(1) Outside-County as Stated on Form 3541	0	0
	(2) In-County as Stated on Form 3541	0	0
	(3) Other Classes Mailed Through the USPS	1	1
e.	Free Distribution Outside the Mail (Carriers or other means)	106	108
f.	Total Free Distribution (Sum of 15d. and 15e.) ►	107	109
g.	Total Distribution (Sum of 15c. and 15f) ►	716	725
h.	Copies not Distributed	777	780
i.	Total (Sum of 15g. and h.) ►	1,493	1,505
j.	Percent Paid and/or Requested Circulation (15c. divided by 15g. times 100)	85%	85%

16. Publication of Statement of Ownership
☑ Publication required. Will be printed in the Winter 2003 issue of this publication. ☐ Publication not required.

17. Signature and Title of Editor, Publisher, Business Manager, or Owner
Susan E. Lewis
VP & Publisher - Periodicals
[signature] Susan Lewis
Date 9/30/03

I certify that all information furnished on this form is true and complete. I understand that anyone who furnishes false or misleading information on this form or who omits material or information requested on the form may be subject to criminal sanctions (including fines and imprisonment) and/or civil sanctions (including civil penalties).

Instructions to Publishers

1. Complete and file one copy of this form with your postmaster annually on or before October 1. Keep a copy of the completed form for your records.

2. In cases where the stockholder or security holder is a trustee, include in items 10 and 11 the name of the person or corporation for whom the trustee is acting. Also include the names and addresses of individuals who are stockholders who own or hold 1 percent or more of the total amount of bonds, mortgages, or other securities of the publishing corporation. In item 11, if none, check the box. Use blank sheets if more space is required.

3. Be sure to furnish all circulation information called for in item 15. Free circulation must be shown in items 15d, e, and f.

4. Item 15h., Copies not Distributed, must include (1) newsstand copies originally stated on Form 3541, and returned to the publisher, (2) estimated returns from news agents, and (3), copies for office use, leftovers, spoiled, and all other copies not distributed.

5. If the publication had Periodicals authorization as a general or requester publication, this Statement of Ownership, Management, and Circulation must be published; it must be printed in any issue in October or, if the publication is not published during October, the first issue printed after October.

6. In item 16, indicate the date of the issue in which this Statement of Ownership will be published.

7. Item 17 must be signed.

Failure to file or publish a statement of ownership may lead to suspension of Periodicals authorization.

PS Form 3526, October 1999 (Reverse)